The Templars

The Templars

The Secret History Revealed

Barbara Frale

Foreword by Umberto Eco

Translated from the Italian by Gregory Conti

Arcade Publishing • New York

FIRST ENGLISH-LANGUAGE EDITION

First published in Italy as *I Templari* by Società editrici Il Mulino and
revised for this edition

Library of Congress Cataloging-in-Publication Data

Frale, Barbara.
    [Templari. English]
    The Templars : the secret history revealed / Barbara Frale ; translated from
the Italian by Gregory Conti. —1st English-language ed.
        p. cm.
    Includes bibliographical references.
    ISBN 978-1-55970-889-0 (alk. paper)
    1. Templars — History. 2. Military religious orders — History. 3. Orders
of knighthood and chivalry — History. I. Title.

    CR4743.F6213 2009
    929.7'1 — dc22   2008031201

Published in the United States by Arcade Publishing, Inc., New York
Distributed by Hachette Book Group USA

Visit our Web site at www.arcadepub.com

10 9 8 7 6 5 4 3 2 1

Designed by API

EB

PRINTED IN THE UNITED STATES OF AMERICA

To Salvatore Maracino,
and his big, free Bolognese heart

Contents

III: The Templar Code of Honor

IV: In Service to the Holy Land

V: Between a Rock and a Hard Place: The Papacy, Philip the Fair, and Jacques de Molay

Foreword

The Order of the Knights Templar was dissolved by Pope Clement V at the beginning of the fourteenth century. From its humble beginnings, this society of warrior-monks grew into an extraordinary military and financial power. Eventually, a king wanted to get rid of this order, which had become a state within a state. He selected the appropriate inquisitors, who gathered random rumors about the order and composed a terrible mosaic: depraved crimes, unmentionable heresies, corruption, and a dash of homosexuality thrown in for good measure. The state, at the direction of the inquisitors, arrested and tortured the suspects. He who confessed and repented saved his life; he who declared himself innocent ended up on the scaffold. Finally, the king confiscated the immense properties of the order. This, in sum, was the process King Philip IV of France, also known as Philip the Fair, implemented against the Knights Templar.

And the Templar myth was born. Many at the time were deeply shaken by the concentrated attack on and subsequent demise of the Templars. Beyond sensing its injustice, as was the case even with the great poet Dante, many today remain fascinated by the secret practices attributed to the Templars and wonder about the vast majority of knights who did not die at the stake but simply vanished when the order was disbanded. Contrary to the conclusion that they went into hiding, built lives for themselves, and maintained their silence, there is the more sensational fictional interpretation: they went underground and continued their activities for seven centuries — and are still among us.

There are numerous books on the Templars. The only problem is that in 90 percent of the cases (I correct myself, 99 percent), they are pure fantasy. No other subject has ever inspired more hacks from more countries throughout time than the Templars. There are countless books about their continuous rebirth and their constant presence behind the scenes of history — among the Gnostic sects, satanic fraternities, spiritualists, Pythagorean orders, Rosicrucians, enlightened Masons, and the Priory of Sion. Sometimes these efforts are so obvious that the reader endowed with common sense can enjoy these books as the historical fiction that they are, as with *The Da Vinci Code*, which mimics and reworks all the previous literature on the subject. But we must be careful, because thousands of gullible readers then visit the site of another historical hoax, the town of Rennes-le-Chateau. The only way to determine if a book on the Templars is serious is to check if it ends in 1314, the year their last grand master was burned at the stake.

Arcade is publishing in English for the first time a thoughtful and welcome antidote to these literary frauds: *The Templars* by Barbara Frale, a Vatican Secret Archives historian and scholar who dedicated years of research and writing to this subject. This is a book we have been waiting for, a terrific, entertaining read backed by solid scholarship. Frale is not scandalized by some of the later aspects of the Templar myth. In fact, she views some of the fictional developments with sympathy, but only because they can lead to new, serious research on obscure aspects of the real history of the Templars. For example, is there really a connection between the Templars and the cult of the Holy Grail? It is a theory not to be dismissed, given that a Templar contemporary, Wolfram von Eschenbach, told fables about it. But I would note that poets, as Horace can attest, are allowed some license, and a scholar from the next millennium who discovers one of today's movies that attributes the discovery of the Ark of the Covenant to a certain Indiana Jones would not have good reason to draw from this entertaining invention any conclusions that are historically correct.

Barbara Frale's stunning discovery of the long-lost Chinon Parchment in the Vatican Secret Archives allows us to see in a new light the church's role in the process against the Templars. When Clement V disbanded the order in 1312, he forbade any attempt to restore it without papal consent, threatening with excommunication anyone who uses the name and the distinguishing symbols of the Temple (in 1780, Joseph de Maistre used this very argument against the neo-Templarists of his time). The Order of the Knights Templar was recognized by the Roman Catholic Church and by the various European states, and as such it was formally dissolved at the beginning of the fourteenth century. Here is Barbara Frale's fascinating account of the medieval world's most powerful military order, one that continues to captivate the popular imagination.

—Umberto Eco
Translated by Alessandra Bastagli

The Templars

The Discovery

At its height, the Order of the Knights Templar rivaled the kingdoms of Europe in military might, economic power, and political influence. For seven hundred years the tragic end of this religious military order amid accusations of heresy has been shadowed by controversy, in part because the record of the Templar leadership's trial by the Inquisition — which held the key to the truth — was lost.

In September 2001, I was reading for the thousandth time the inventory of documents on the trial of the Templars in the Vatican Secret Archives. It's no exaggeration to say I knew it by heart, having studied it since 1994, while I was at the Vatican School of Paleography, and countless times during my four years in the doctoral program at the University of Venice. But it wasn't until that day that I noticed a most curious fact in one particular document: at the diocesan inquest in Tours, one of the many local hearings throughout Christendom that Pope Clement V had ordered to be held on the Templars, the questioning was directed by Cardinal Bérenger Frédol. There was something very odd about that.

The cardinal was an eminent canon lawyer, a papal legate for the most delicate diplomatic missions, a prominent member of the College of Cardinals, and a nephew of Clement V. Could a person of such stature actually take his leave from the Curia, the central governing body of the Roman Catholic Church, and head off to some provincial backwater to direct one of the hundreds of diocesan inquests?

A closer examination immediately made everything clear. This was no ordinary diocesan inquest. This was a hearing held by three plenipotentiaries — or representatives invested with full power or authority — of Clement V in the secret quarters of the castle of Chinon concerning Grand Master Jacques de Molay and other leaders of the Order of the Knights Templar. King Philip IV of France had sequestered the Templar leadership there in order to keep them from meeting with the pope. This was the very trial that had been in dispute for so many years. Because all the evidence for the trial had come from indirect sources, many questioned whether it had actually taken place. The document, known as the Chinon Parchment, had always been in the Vatican Secret Archives, but in 1628, it had been cataloged merely as a record of an inquest "in the diocese of Tours." This was an accurate classification at the time, because in that period Chinon Castle was in the diocese of Tours. For modern scholars, however, the description was incomplete and misleading, so the true historic relevance of the Chinon Parchment remained unrecognized for nearly four hundred years — until that day in September 2001.

A close reading of the text left no doubt. The Chinon Parchment is the record of the trial of the Templar leadership by the pope's personal representatives. It contains details of the order's secret initiation ceremony, which had fueled great scandal. More important, it reveals that the grand master and other high-ranking Templars were found innocent of the charges of heresy, were absolved for less serious offenses by the apostolic authority, and were fully reintegrated into the Catholic community. Historians believed that the Templars were innocent of the charges brought against them by Philip IV, but many outside academia still suspected the Templars of having been heretics and occultists. The Chinon Parchment is the definitive and incontrovertible proof of the Templars' innocence, and should finally put this question to rest.

This book reexamines the medieval world's most powerful military order in light of this groundbreaking new information. In the pages that follow, I trace the religious, sociocultural, and political developments that gave rise to the Templars, their remarkable ascendance, their many achievements, and the struggle for dominance between church and state that ultimately led to their spectacular fall. I begin by assuming the perspective of a Christian at that time to introduce some of the commonly held beliefs and traditions of medieval Christendom, from which the Templars sprang.

I

Jerusalem, the Holy Sepulchre, and the Temple

Alpha and Omega — Beginning and End

Jesus, son of Mary, died in Jerusalem on April 7 in the year 790 after the founding of Rome, the nineteenth year of the reign of Emperor Tiberius. His disciples, who had come from the surrounding areas to follow him, were in a state of despair over the loss of their leader. But they soon resumed their religious activities with renewed enthusiasm, because they were certain that their master had risen from the dead as had been foretold.

While the Roman citizen Saul of Tarsus spread the message of the new Christian doctrine throughout the Greco-Hellenic world, and the former fisherman Simon Peter evangelized the capital of the empire and founded the Church of Rome, the disciples who remained in and around Jerusalem gathered up all the evidence of Christ's earthly passage and began preparing a well-ordered record of the events of his life, death, and resurrection in accounts that bore the auspicious title that Jesus himself had suggested: Good News, or the Gospel.

The Christian community of Jerusalem had carefully marked the locations where Jesus' teaching and sacrifice had taken place, especially those connected with his death, so they would be able to recognize and venerate them through the ages. According to one tradition, after the prodigious events announced by the Scriptures had come to pass, the master's mother herself was the first to revisit all the places of his suffering and death in Jerusalem, celebrating with this painful commemoration a symbolic pilgrimage to the most important sites of the new faith.

The persecution unleashed by the Romans against the Christians of Jerusalem forced many of them to flee to surrounding areas and made it advisable to move the most cherished relics to a safer place; these were considered the signs of a tangible legacy Christ left to his distraught followers as an act of mercy, so that they would persist in their faith.

In the fourth century, the emperor Constantine converted to Christianity and fostered its growth within the Roman Empire. The empress mother Helen — more sincere in her religious choices than her son, who had embraced Christianity primarily for political reasons — dedicated her energy to a painstaking exploration of the city of Jerusalem in search of any physical traces of Christ. She conducted what amounted to an archaeological expedition, studying the ancient documents and local traditions before excavating to bring to light vestiges of Christ's life and death. The result was the discovery of the wood of the

True Cross and other important and powerfully evocative relics.

Constantine ordered the construction of the glorious Basilica of the Anastasis (Resurrection), also known as the Church of the Holy Sepulchre, on the actual site of the garden of Joseph of Arimathea, where the body of Christ had been laid to rest and where the resurrection had taken place. Since then, Christians from East and West have never stopped flocking to Palestine in search of answers to their own spiritual questions, hungry for physical contact with the tomb of Christ and eager to breathe in the aura of holiness that envelops Jerusalem, the City of God.

During the seventh century, the Arabs wrested the region from the Byzantine emperors, and Jerusalem came under Muslim rule, which, after the violent phase of the conquest had ended, maintained an attitude of relative tolerance toward the Christian religion and its sacred sites. Christians were obliged to pay a special tax based on their status as foreign infidels (*dhimmi*), but they were allowed to continue practicing their religion. When Charlemagne founded the Holy Roman Empire in the year 800, he took it upon himself to safeguard as much as possible the Christian population of Jerusalem under Muslim domination. The empire's skillful diplomats succeeded in negotiating a treaty with the caliph of Baghdad, Harun al-Rashid, which officially recognized Charlemagne as the Protector of the Holy Sepulchre. Christian pilgrimages to Jerusalem continued unhindered for over two hundred years.

At the beginning of the eleventh century, Palestine passed into the control of the Fatimid caliph of Egypt, bringing an end to the long period of relative peace. In 1009, in a terrible reawakening of fanaticism, the Muslim authorities in Syria ordered the sack of Jerusalem and the destruction of the Holy Sepulchre, launching a concerted assault on the sacred sites of Christianity. News of the devastation provoked an outcry in the West, but pilgrimages to the Holy Land did not come to a halt. On the contrary, religious traffic to Jerusalem intensified substantially, as though awareness that the trip had become dangerous made it an even more heroic and worthy undertaking.

The medieval chronicler Rudolph Glaber and other writers of the time wondered what might explain this unusual number of pilgrims who left everything behind to go to the Holy Land. They were convinced that a supernatural force was driving people to undertake the perilous journey, and not only public sinners who had to atone for grave sins or outcasts who had no place in society, but even great feudal lords who took a leap into the unknown, abandoning a life of privilege in their homelands. Between 1026 and 1065, many noblemen, including William, count of Angoulême, Robert the Magnificent, duke of Normandy, and Gunther of Bamberg, set out for Jerusalem, each bringing an entourage of faithful followers and armed men.

The new outbreaks of violence that swept through the Holy Land toward the end of the century shocked the collective consciousness of Europe. It was as though evil itself, identified as the pagan invader and profaner, was unleashing on the Christian people the final attack that was the harbinger of the end of the world.

There was an old prophecy. In his *Libellus de Anticristo*, Abbot Adso of Montier-en-Der (910–92) had foretold that the last king of the Franks, he who held all the power of the Roman Empire, would journey to Jerusalem and lay down his scepter and crown on the Mount of Olives. This would announce the end of time, which would culminate in the coming of the Antichrist and Judgment Day. The dramatic events in the East had breathed new life into this prophecy, and European public opinion was convinced of the need to journey to the City of God to await the end of days and participate in the mystery of redemption.

The warnings of ancient scripture echoed in the minds of the people. The fear that the world was coming to an end, briefly put to rest by the midnight bells sounding the start of the year 1000, still had a profound hold on the masses through the words of Revelation:

> And I saw the holy city, the new Jerusalem, coming down out of heaven from God, made ready as a bride adorned for her husband. Behold, the tabernacle of God is among men, and He will dwell among them, and they shall be His people, and God Himself will be among them, and He will wipe away every tear from their eyes. . . . I am the Alpha and the Omega, the beginning and the end.

Take Back the Promised Land

For centuries, the Byzantine emperors considered themselves the protectors of Jerusalem and the Holy Land. They negotiated treaties with the Muslim governors of the city for the restoration of the Church of the Holy Sepulchre after its destruction in 1009, and effectively used diplomacy to ensure better treatment for the Christians who resided there.

In 1054 substantial theological, political, and cultural differences between the Eastern (Greek) and Western (Latin) branches of Christendom culminated in a permanent rupture when the patriarch of the Byzantine capital of Constantinople Michael Cerularius refused to recognize the primacy of Pope Leo IX (1048–54) as head of the church. The Great Schism divided the Christian world into the Eastern Orthodox Church and the Roman Catholic Church, a traumatic break subsequent popes labored to heal.

In 1071 the Turks routed the troops of the Byzantine emperor Alexius Comnenus at the battle of Manzikert. After inflicting this crushing defeat on the Christians, they extended their power throughout the Middle East. The arrival of the Turkish conquerors threw Palestine into a state of anarchy and chaos. The Greek patriarch Simeon, who lived in Jerusalem, left the city, together with his clerics, and withdrew to the nearby island of Cyprus. Pilgrimages became extremely dangerous, because the roads were infested with Muslim brigands who kidnapped and often brutally murdered wayfarers.

Emperor Alexius Comnenus faced a second challenge from the Normans, who conquered Bari and were aiming to take from Byzantine control a vast area of territory in southern Italy. Attacked on two fronts by different enemies and worried by the spread of Turkish power in the Eastern empire, Alexius appealed for help several times to Pope Gregory VII (1073–85), asking him to incite the population of Western Christendom to undertake the journey to the Holy Land and reinforce Byzantine imperial troops against the Muslim advance.

At that time, the Church of Rome was in the midst of a crisis. Between the reigns of Pope Stephen VI (896–97) and Pope John XII (955–64), the papacy had fallen under the domination of the powerful families of the Roman aristocracy and the scandalous intrigues of the noblewoman Marozia, who determined the elections and the policies of a succession of popes notable only for their unabashed immorality and corruption. The German emperor Otto III endeavored to reform the church and restore order. He engineered the election of Gerbert d'Aurillac, his scholarly mentor, as Pope Sylvester II, and supported the new pope in addressing the crisis. Otto III's death in 1002 did not halt the reform process, which was carried on by succeeding popes and completed under Pope Gregory VII.

Gregory VII was a proud defender of papal supremacy, which was rooted in the role of the bishop of Rome as the direct successor of Saint Peter, designated by Christ himself as the head of his church. The pope struggled against the interference of Holy Roman emperor Henry IV in ecclesiastic affairs and the flagrant insubordination of many bishops who aligned themselves with the emperor. It was while he was engaged in confronting this political opposition within the church that the pope received the Byzantine emperor's appeal for help against the Turks. The pope called on the feudal lords who had taken a solemn oath of loyalty to the papacy to participate in a military expedition.

The mission inevitably meant that not only would the lords be away from their homelands for months, if not years, during which time their families and estates would be subject to aggression and thievery, but that they would endanger life and limb in the battle against the Turks. To compensate for these earthly risks, the pope extended to all who were ready to obey him a special blessing of the church. He proclaimed that the military mission would be a service to Saint Peter himself and that the participants would profit from the dual advantage of the material goods they would seize from the infidels and eternal life in heaven. Gregory VII decided that he would personally lead this aid expedition, but he died in 1085 without having successfully organized it.

From 1085 to 1095, a series of natural disasters and famines struck Europe, recalling the ancient prophecies of the coming of the Antichrist and leading many to believe that the end of the world was at hand. In 1089 and 1094 two terrible epidemics of Saint Anthony's Fire — fungal poisoning that causes burning sensations in limbs, gangrene, and ultimately death — swept through rural Germany. In Rathsbone and Bavaria the disease killed more than eight thousand in twelve weeks. A group of bishops returning from the city of Mainz saw the church in one village so crammed with dead bodies that the bishops couldn't get in the door. According to medieval belief, such scourges served a spiritual purpose: to turn the people of God toward penitence and redemption. A plethora of supernatural signs inspired the masses to repent: sightings of comets, eclipses, celestial wonders, and mysterious crosses that formed on the backs of those who had fallen in the service of God, thus manifesting their salvation.

Liberate the Holy Sepulchre, Bring Peace to Europe

Odo de Lagery was born into a French noble family and received an excellent education at the parochial school in Reims. When he was twenty-eight, he entered the monastery in Cluny. Sent to Rome, he quickly distinguished himself and was named cardinal and bishop of Ostia. Pope Gregory VII had deeply appreciated Odo's service during his difficult struggle for reform and made him one of his closest personal advisers in the last years of his papacy. In March 1088, Odo was elected pope and took the name of

Urban II. A highly capable man gifted with a courteous manner and persuasive eloquence, Urban II had considerable diplomatic experience and was skilled in building consensus.

In the early months of 1095, Urban II left Rome and invited the rulers of Western Christendom to join him in the city of Piacenza, where he held the first great council of his papacy. There, the pope discussed the many serious questions confronting the church, including the scourge of simony (the buying and selling of religious offices) and the recently revealed adultery of King Philip I of France, whom history would remember as Philip the Amorous.

A delegation of ambassadors from the Byzantine emperor arrived with a renewed request for military support. The situation was becoming increasingly dire because Constantinople did not have enough troops to defend the vast territories of its empire, and the Turkish menace had once again forced a state of emergency. The ambassadors were clever men who knew exactly what chords to strike to appeal to the pontiff's sympathies. They related accounts of atrocities suffered by Christians in Jerusalem at the hands of the Turks. The envoys also assured the pope that Emperor Alexius Comnenus would be so grateful for his commitment to recruit Western soldiers as reinforcements to the Byzantine army that relations between the Church of Constantinople and the Church of Rome would benefit greatly.

The emperor was reaching out to the pope not only

to ask for help but to propose an act of reconciliation. But the pope had other pressing concerns. Europe was undergoing a prolonged period of political instability that dated back to the Treaty of Verdun. In 846 the treaty brought an end to the unity of the Holy Roman Empire, dividing it among Charlemagne's heirs and ushering in a phase of decline marked by terrifying incursions by the Hungarians, Normans, and Saracens.

During the tenth century, in those areas where the decline of imperial authority had been more rapid, such as south-central France, small local potentates had emerged to fill the vacuum, often usurping power through barely legal, sometimes openly illegal, means. These opportunists were professionals of war on horseback, armed to the teeth with steel, who instilled fear in the masses of peasants and artisans. Clothed with the title of *milites* (soldiers), they were in perennial conflict among themselves for control of territory and were often involved in bitter clashes with the legitimate representatives of the central authorities. They were sometimes allied with the noble descendants of former officials of the empire, whose families had preserved their wealth and social prominence. These roving bands of armed men were a constant threat to the tranquillity of rural communities. They destroyed crops, plundered villages, and killed defenseless peasants and townspeople — even priests — often without any better reason than the desire for loot. Many were the younger sons of noble families, who were disadvantaged by the ancient tradition of primogeniture, the sole right of the firstborn son to inherit the entirety of his father's titles, estates, and wealth.

According to the papal records of Gregory VII, in 1074 the knight Lancelin de Beaugency, the leader of an armed band, ambushed and robbed the archbishop of Tours while the prelate was on a pilgrimage to Rome. The bishop of Liège was the victim of a similar assault in 1080 at the hands of the count of Chiny. Three years later, in the French diocese of Terouanne, the knight Oilard and Count Eustache broke down the door of the cathedral, profaned the relics, stole all the valuable decorations, and dragged off Bishop Lambert, whom they found lying prostrate in prayer, and mutilated him.

The church did everything in its power to limit such episodes, but even the threat of excommunication resulted in only a temporary cessation. Local bishops had tried to curtail the violence by obliging these knights to take solemn oaths of peace, so that at least the poor, the defenseless, and religious orders would be spared from their brutality. "Truces of God" were called repeatedly throughout the course of the eleventh century in the hopes of putting a halt to the rampant looting and murder, to no avail. The solemn promises of peace were inevitably followed by new outbreaks of carnage, and the church's condemnation of the perpetrators was never enough to put a stop to the destruction.

In November 1095, Urban II was in Clermont to preside over a council called to declare yet another truce of

God about which, given past experience, he was not very optimistic. The Byzantine emperor's request for Western troops to help block the Turkish advance presented the perfect solution to an incessant problem: the bands of knights terrorizing Europe could be sent to the Holy Land and encouraged to unleash all their violence against the infidels who were massacring Christians in the East and profaning Christian holy sites.

On the last day of the Council of Clermont, having addressed all the issues on the agenda, Urban II called upon all of his powers of persuasion to launch an unprecedented undertaking. Crusade!

In attendance were knights, mercenaries, and veterans of war. The pope had no illusions about these violent groups of armed men who had so disturbed the peace. He calibrated his speech to appeal to their baser natures, emphasizing all the material advantages they would reap from the expedition. Recapturing the Holy Land from the Turks amounted to the creation of another homeland and the assurance of a prestigious social position for all those without one in the lands of Western Christendom. The pope spoke of the possibility of winning a rich booty from the infidels and of establishing new fiefdoms that could become permanent settlements. But the war against the Muslim foe promised something infinitely more profound: it meant defeating the enemies of Christ and the butchers of Europe's Christian brothers and sisters.

Urban II urged the young nobles and the military men

present at the council to leave home and volunteer as auxiliary soldiers in service to the Byzantine emperor. Their response was completely unforeseen.

"*Venerunt Gentes*" (*The Heathen Have Come*)

The pope announced that on the following Tuesday, November 27, 1095, he would make a special proclamation. That day, so many gathered to hear him that they could not fit inside the cathedral. The papal throne had to be mounted on a platform in an open field outside the eastern gate of the city of Clermont. Several versions of his speech have come down to us, but all appeared many years after the actual event, so we do not know for certain what his exact words were. We *do* know that the crowd that had assembled was overcome with wild enthusiasm and repeatedly interrupted his speech with shouts of "God wills it."

The bishop of Le Puy threw himself at the pope's feet and was the first to ask to join the crusade. Cardinal Gregory dropped to his knees to recite the Confiteor, a prayer of confession, and the entire crowd echoed his words. However, it was decided that priests could not participate in the crusade without permission from their bishops, women could not go on their own, and newlywed husbands would be discouraged from volunteering to ensure the continuity of the family.

In the months that followed, a monk known as Peter

the Hermit, who had been a pilgrim to Jerusalem and who moved listeners with his account of the persecution of Christians in the Holy Land, ventured east from the French region of Berry in search of new recruits for the crusade. By the time he arrived in the German city of Cologne he had mobilized some fifteen thousand people, and still more came from other parts of Germany.

Urban II continued preaching crusade with great energy, making his way across France in a series of synods, or assemblies, in Limoges, Poitiers, Angers, Le Mans, Saintes, Bourdeaux, Toulouse, and Nîmes. His appeal resounded beyond the borders of France and inflamed all of Europe. It launched an intense reawakening of popular devotion. There were waves of conversions and a massive increase in the number of pilgrims to Jerusalem from every corner of Western Christiandom, who intoned the lament of Psalm 78:

> O God, the heathen have come to invade thy inheritance;
> They have defiled your holy temple,
> They have laid Jerusalem in ruins

Those of modest standing set off immediately on the voyage. The great lords and nobles left only after they had taken the necessary steps to safeguard their families and their properties. Although these enjoyed the solemn protection of the church, the uncertain times suggested more concrete precautions.

The crusade was a complex phenomenon; it was responsible for an outpouring of faith that involved all of European society, inspiring the masses and profoundly influencing the work of the most prominent intellectuals. Some members of the military class considered the expedition a welcome and useful period of service in arms, which compensated for the forced inactivity that followed truces of God. But there were many others who, emulating noble lords such as William of Angoulême and Gunther of Bamberg, left their homes resolved on forging an indissoluble bond with the Holy Land — perhaps even to die there and be buried beside the Holy Sepulchre.

Constant Risk

The crusade unfolded as a series of expeditions led by noblemen that reached Palestine independently by sea or by land. On July 15, 1099, after a terrible siege, the crusaders finally recaptured Jerusalem, one of the greatest fortresses of the medieval world — but not without some committing heinous crimes at the expense of the Muslim population, despite orders from their leaders to protect those who had surrendered.

On July 22, Godfrey de Bouillon, duke of Lorraine, one of the leaders of the crusade, became the first ruler of the Kingdom of Jerusalem. Godfrey refused the title of king and instead asked to be called *Advocatus Sancti Sepulchri*, or Defender of the Holy Sepulchre. Less than a year into his reign, he contracted an illness and died. On Christmas Day 1100, Godfrey was succeeded by his brother Baldwin I, who was crowned king by the patriarch of Jerusalem, the highest-ranking member of the church hierarchy in the Holy Land.

By then, the Christian territories in the Holy Land were organized into three states that occupied a narrow coastal strip and were anything but united: the Kingdom of Jerusalem in the south and the Principality of Antioch and the County of Edessa in the north. Lacking a central government, the crusaders — who were known as Franks because most of them hailed from France — established garrisons in strategic locations, where they could exact tribute from nearby villages and enhance their revenues through profitable raids into bordering lands.

Baldwin I was immediately faced with two pressing problems: insufficient troops and a small Christian population. As the youngest of three brothers, Baldwin was unable to bring his own retinue of soldiers and followers when he left for the crusade, and only inherited those of his brother's followers who chose not to return to Europe. The contingent of knights at his disposal was composed of pious men who had taken a vow to remain forever in the Holy Land and adventurers who had come for profit — too few to constitute an effective and dependable army.

Under the Byzantine Empire, Antioch had been a wealthy city, strategically situated in a land of plentiful natural resources and further enriched by trade and the manufacture of prestigious products. After the Christian conquest, the crusader prince Bohemond of Taranto established control over the city and declared it an independent principality. The County of Edessa served mainly as a buffer state to protect Antioch from attacks by its Muslim neighbors. It was populated by a highly diverse blend of races and cultures, including Syrian and Armenian Christians as well as Arabs.

Despite occupying most of Palestine, the crusaders were unable to exercise complete control over the territory, and they were constantly exposed to the risk of Muslim aggression. Their most dangerous enemy was the Fatimid caliph of Egypt, who controlled garrisons in the coastal cities of Gaza and Ashkelon south of Jerusalem, and was ready to join forces with the Bedouins, who could enter Palestine by skirting the Dead Sea on trails from Arabia. The Egyptians maintained political relations with the emirs of Arsuf and Caesarea, even though the emirs had signed acts of submission to the king of Jerusalem. The entire network of roads in the Holy Land was overrun with Egyptian brigands from the south, Bedouins from the east, and Muslim refugees from the north, all of whom robbed and often killed travelers.

Palestine was arid and poor in natural resources, and the lifestyles of the new arrivals from Europe, who were accustomed to abundant food and inadequate hygiene, led to increased mortality rates, especially among infants.

In 1101 another expedition from the West arrived to bolster the weak Christian states in the Holy Land. With these reinforcements, the Christians managed to conquer Tripoli and other lands previously under Arab control, which held great strategic value for the survival of the realm. The captured territories created a safe corridor for Christian troops to move freely between Jerusalem and the northern outposts of Edessa and Antioch.

Despite this, by 1115 a beleaguered Baldwin I launched an appeal for Eastern Christians to emigrate to the Holy Land to buttress its flagging population. Control of the road network was vital, both for collecting tolls from commercial convoys arriving from eastern sea routes and for ensuring the safety of pilgrims to the sacred sites, the spiritual heart of the realm.

Sentinels

The care of the souls of the Christian faithful and the celebration of the liturgy at the Church of the Holy Sepulchre, were carried out by priests from Europe who practiced the Latin rite of the Roman Church. They joined the clergy of the Greek rite, which had been established by the Byzantine emperors centuries earlier at the church. These monks never left Jerusalem, even during the harshest periods of

Muslim domination. They continued to reside at the church and to celebrate the Eastern liturgy at an altar reserved for them.

Al-Aqsa mosque, built on the ruins of the Temple of Solomon, was known as the Dome of the Rock because it contained the block of stone from which the prophet Mohammed is believed to have ascended into heaven. The mosque was converted to a church, in which Augustinian priests regularly celebrated the liturgy, and referred to by its original name, the Temple. Both the Temple and the Holy Sepulchre were home to knights who had taken a vow to live with the priests and in keeping with the Augustinian rule, while maintaining their membership in the military aristocracy. This lay brotherhood served the needs of the churches to obtain remission of their sins.

The group that dedicated itself to the Temple was led by Hugh de Payens, a French knight who was lord of a small fief in Troyes. We cannot be sure if Payens participated in the first crusade and the conquest of Jerusalem. What is certain is that in 1104 or 1105, he arrived in the Holy Land in the entourage of Hugh, count of Champagne, who was on his first pilgrimage. In 1113, Payens was back in France, but he returned to Jerusalem in 1114 and remained there without interruption for several years. He may have been widowed after his last stay in the Holy City, which would have enabled him to strengthen his religious commitment — an impossibility had he been married.

On Easter 1119, three hundred pilgrims who had traveled from Jerusalem to the banks of the Jordan River were massacred by Saracens. The news sent shock waves through Europe and figured prominently in the chronicle of the historian Albert of Aix. The following year, an important assembly of Christian leaders was held captive by Muslims in the city of Nablus. King Baldwin II of Jerusalem launched a new appeal to the Christian faithful, emphasizing that the Holy Land was in desperate need of a greater protective force.

The rulers of the other Christian states often demonstrated their independence from the king of Jerusalem, but Baldwin II could not curtail their power because he relied on their forces for the protection of the kingdom. Baldwin II and the patriarch of Jerusalem, the wise and humble Garmond of Picquigny, concluded that the solution to this problem lay in the brotherhood of soldiers founded by Hugh de Payens. An independent order of knights subject only to the church and loyal to the king of Jerusalem would free Baldwin II of his dependence on the often quarrelsome and rebellious lords of the realm.

In 1120 or thereabouts, according to the chronicle of William, archbishop of Tyre, Hugh de Payens and his comrades took the three monastic vows of chastity, poverty, and obedience before the patriarch of Jerusalem, who officially entrusted them with the mission of protecting Christian pilgrims from Muslim attack.

Baldwin II gave Hugh de Payens and his knights a wing of the building he had formerly used as his royal palace, near the ruins of the Temple of Solomon. The members of the brotherhood were called the Knights of the Temple of Solomon, and later, Brothers of the Temple or the Templars.

II

An Order of Holy Warriors

The Powerful Take Interest

Hugh de Payens wanted his brotherhood to be distinguished by its devotion to the values of poverty and penitence. At the beginning of the twelfth century, poverty meant something quite different from what it means today. Primarily a spiritual rather than material quality, poverty was the mark of the defenseless and represented a moral value. *Poor* was not the opposite of *rich* but rather the opposite of *potent*, which referred to military and social power. To be poor was to be humble or powerless; it did not equate to economic need.

In the social context of the early twelfth century, secular power lay with those who bore arms — and those who commanded them. Since the early centuries of Christianity, public sinners who had committed grievous acts such as murder, adultery, and apostasy were obliged by religious authorities to renounce arms forever, among other forms of penance. There were those who, although completely innocent of such crimes, voluntarily subjected themselves to the same program of atonement as an act of piety.

To freely renounce military power — and the dominance over others that came with it — was to willingly choose a life of poverty.

The highly personal and modest nature of Hugh de Payens's proposed rule for his brotherhood was in sharp contrast to the needs of Baldwin II, who was faced with a dwindling Christian population and the lack of a dependable military force capable of defending it — a situation that seriously threatened the continued survival of the Christian states in the Holy Land. The establishment of a true military order would mean not only recruiting a significant number of soldiers but also finding the vast economic resources necessary to maintain the army, ensure adequate provisions, and procure all of the requisite equipment. In a world where war was waged primarily on horseback, with knights outfitted in expensive suits of armor that were the product of long months of work by specialized craftsmen, the military corps that Baldwin II envisioned could never be truly poor.

Hugh de Payens, as founder and head of the order, would have to take on substantial administrative, legal, and military responsibilities similar to those he had exercised in his secular life as lord of his fief in Troyes — the very responsibilities he had renounced to live in Jerusalem as a penitent brother in the Temple of Solomon.

It may be that the visit by Count Fulk of Anjou to the Templars in 1120 and his decision to live with them for an extended period was not a chance event unrelated to the larger designs of the king of Jerusalem. That year, Baldwin II donated to the order their headquarters, a residence ill suited to the group's original vow of poverty but which held great symbolic value. Accepting that donation demonstrated that the nature of the order was changing and that it was assuming a privileged role in the Holy Land on behalf of the king.

In bringing pressure to bear on the first Templars, the crown must have had the support of the patriarch of Jerusalem, who shared the king's concern for the defense of the realm. At that time, the brotherhood was subject to the patriarch, and it was probably Garmond of Picquigny who ultimately convinced Payens to undertake the radical transformation of the order to serve the needs of the kingdom. The Order of the Knights Hospitaller of Saint John, founded in Jerusalem and recognized by the pope in 1113, was a brotherhood devoted to the care of the sick. Like the Templars, the Hospitallers were asked to assume a military function completely at odds with their original vocation.

Overcoming the reluctance of the original Templars was not the king's only obstacle. The population of the kingdom could not satisfy the order's need for new recruits; these had to come from elsewhere. And while Baldwin II had the support of the patriarch of Jerusalem, he could not institute a new religious order without the approval of the pope.

In 1126, Hugh de Payens's feudal lord, Hugh, count of Champagne, returned to Jerusalem and joined the Templars.

A powerful man, he belonged to one of the most eminent noble families of France and had political connections throughout Europe. The following year, Payens and several comrades journeyed to the West, where the fate of the order would be decided. On his way to France, he probably made a stop in Rome, where he requested an audience with Honorius II (1124–30), a pope sensitive to the problems of the Holy Land, who surely would have shown interest in the proposed religious order. From 1127 to 1130, with the assistance of his fellow knights from various regions of France, Payens traveled around Europe, making contact with influential people. He stopped in his native region of Champagne, then proceeded to Anjou and La Maine, where he had excellent relations with Count Fulk V. He went to Poitou and Normandy, where he was welcomed by King Henry I, who sent him, under royal patronage, to England and Scotland. Payens returned to France, visited Flanders, and traveled down the Rhone Valley to Marseille. By the time he embarked on his trip back to Jerusalem, he had recruited a substantial number of new Templars.

Institutional Problems

In January 1129 the papal legate, Cardinal Matthew of Albano, was in France to take part in the Council of Troyes. Originally convened to declare a truce of God, the council provided an excellent opportunity to discuss the proposed religious military order of the Templars.

Both the church and the nobility with legitimate rights of lordship, exposed to the constant risk of social disorder from marauding knights, saw the new religious order as a way of institutionalizing the crusading experience. Knights who were mercenaries or who had no established role in society and often lived as bandits would be able to invest their energies in serving an honorable cause. The church, the noble lords of Europe against whom these bands of knights so often rebelled, and the population that was victimized by their abuses would certainly benefit from their departure for the Holy Land. In light of this situation, it is easier to understand the generosity of spirit with which the great feudal lords welcomed Hugh de Payens and the idea of a military order, as well as the conspicuous number of recruits he drew during his travels.

The Templars were not simply a military corps guided by religious values. Merely expanding and institutionalizing Payens's military brotherhood meant risking the possibility that the future army would come under the control of some secular power or of the military aristocracy from which its members came. To ensure its deployment for the exclusive benefit of the Holy Land, it had to be autonomous from all civil authority and subject only to the church, an arrangement that pertained only to monastic orders. But it was an extremely delicate moment in the history of the papacy.

In the period between 1120, when Hugh de Payens and his comrades took their religious vows before Patriarch Garmond of Picquigny, and 1127, when they went on their mission to the West, the papacy found itself under the constant threat of a schism. During the pontificates of Urban II (1088–99) and Paschal II (1099–1118), the Curia, the governing body of the church, had chosen new cardinals from the monastic realm, especially natives of Rome and central and southern Italy, who were more likely to support the ecclesiastical policies instituted by Pope Gregory VII. Pope Callistus II (1119–24), a native of Burgundy, promoted the reorganization of the Curia and adopted a different approach to ecclesiastical policy that privileged the bishops, the Cistercians, and the new religious orders of Augustinians and Premonstratensians. Callistus II favored the selection of men like himself who came from Burgundy. These French clerics, who belonged to the reform orders and concentrated their energies on caring for the souls of the faithful, were seen as innovators and were viewed with a certain apprehension. These competing lines of church policy divided the Curia, which was already characterized by differences of culture and background. The leader of the French contingent was Aymeric of Burgundy, who had been appointed deacon of Santa Maria Nova in 1123 and later elevated to the office of chancellor. He became the decisive authority in the development of papal policy, and during the next two papal elections, with the support of the Frangipani family, he managed to engineer the victories of his candidates.

Upon the death of Callistus II on December 13, 1124, the majority of the College of Cardinals reached agreement on the election of Cardinal Sasso of Saint Stephen's Church in Rome, but the powerful Pierleoni family opposed him, and just three days later, they were able to force the election of Cardinal Theobald of Saint Anastasia, who took the name of Celestine II. But the new pope barely had time to don the red cloak and intone the Te Deum, a hymn of praise, before the Frangipanis burst into the papal apartments with swords drawn, wounding him and forcing him to abdicate. Subsequently, by agreement with Aymeric of Burgundy, Cardinal Lambert Scannabecchi of Ostia was elected Pope Honorius II (1124–30). The Pierleoni family decided to accept his election in exchange for large sums of money and promises of favors.

Honorius II was a staunch defender of papal independence against outside interference from secular powers, a faithful servant of the cause of reforming the church, and a proponent of diplomatic mediation to consolidate the central role of the Holy See. His pontificate, born of the French chancellor's crafty plotting, succeeded for several years in maintaining a truce between the rival factions of the Roman aristocracy for control over the papal throne, but its imminent end raised fears of a difficult succession.

The Moral Question

Hugh de Payens had sought the support of some illustrious religious personalities of his time. In 1128 the Cistercian prior of the Grand-Chartreuse monastery, whom
Hugh had consulted, responded with a rather demoraliz-
ing letter: It is no use attacking outside enemies if you cannot dominate those within, that is, moral vices, and it is
not productive to try to liberate the Holy Land from the
infidels unless you can first liberate your soul from its
shortcomings. Citing a letter from Saint Paul to the Eph-
esians, the prior declared that "indeed it is not against enemies in flesh and blood that we have to fight, but against
the Lords, the Powers, the Rulers of the world of darkness,
against the evil spirits which inhabit the heavens." It was a
spiritual lesson from a man devoted to the contemplative
life who could not imagine what it meant to find oneself
surrounded by a group of Muslim bandits, ready to attack
a company of pilgrims.

Nonetheless, the reservations expressed by the prior
of Grand-Chartreuse were representative of an old and
widely shared way of thinking. Christian morality had always rejected the avowal of war, even though there is no
passage in the Gospels that explicitly condemns it. In early
Christian times, an initiate's military service was regarded
as an act of contempt against the law of God, and there
were those who were later recognized as saints who had
solemnly bid farewell to arms in order to embrace the

Christian life. The question of a just war and the legitimacy of using force had also been addressed, among others, by Saint Ambrose and Saint Augustine, but the subject remained an extremely delicate matter.

However, the grave problems afflicting Western society favored more moderate attitudes toward military solutions on the part of the church. This shift was first evident when Burkard of Worms (965–1025), in his *Decretum*, quoted the letter of Pope Nicholas I (858–67), in which the pope restored to penitents the use of arms if they were necessary in the fight against the pagans. In the early tenth century, the conflict between the papacy and the Holy Roman Empire over the investiture of (or right to appoint) bishops and the church's struggle to free itself from secular interference demonstrated the need for a militia under the pope's command that could be called up to defend the pontiff or to discourage possible aggressors. Pope Gregory VII had gone so far as to bless the service of those knights who volunteered their military acumen for the defense of the church. Those knights, however, were not monks but laymen who had always used the instruments of war and would continue to do so.

The creation of a religious military order stood in stark contrast to an ideal that had dominated Western monastic life for centuries: *contemptus mundi*, or contempt for the world. This idea held that there could be no eternal salvation without a total conversion, which meant abandoning the world and its multiple corrupting forces and embracing the cloister and a life of asceticism. Saint Peter Damian, one of the most important advocates for church reform and an adviser to Pope Gregory VII, condemned the practice of war, holding it incompatible with spiritual perfection, which can be achieved only in the contemplative life. In the period immediately following the first crusade, despite the widespread enthusiasm for the liberation of the Holy Sepulchre, many men of the church still held this view.

There was someone who could help Hugh de Payens in his endeavor to promote the fusion of two ideals judged by much of Christian society to be irreconcilable opposites. Born to a family of chivalric lineage that belonged to the lesser nobility of Burgundy, Bernard of Clairvaux was a renowned abbot and mystic, a man endowed with an uncommon talent for communication but also capable of moving the right levers in both the political and religious spheres. He had voluntarily chosen the way of the cloister at the age of twenty-one, convincing his brothers to follow him. In 1113 he had taken monastic vows to enter the reformed Benedictine community in Citeaux. A powerful advocate of monastic reform, Bernard shared the ideal of *contemptus mundi*.

Hugh de Payens probably called upon Bernard immediately after his arrival in the West. Their families, both members of the lesser nobility, may have been joined by bonds of blood and political alliance. Payens may have presented him with a letter from Baldwin II, asking Bernard to devise an appropriate monastic rule for the Templars, a rule not only suitable to the dignity of a religious order but compatible with the necessity of waging war. Some historians are skeptical about the authenticity of this document, but it is certain that Payens tried to enlist Bernard's help, and that at first he experienced the disappointment of being completely ignored.

The rationale of this new religious order composed of monks devoted to war initially must have seemed absurd to the abbot, something that resembled a monstrous hybrid. Just one or two years before Payens's journey to the West, Bernard had expressed his regret to the count of Champagne regarding the latter's decision to abandon his longtime plan to enter the community of Citeaux in order to become a Templar. Bernard was not a purist like Peter Damian. He knew all too well the way of life of the secular knighthood, having belonged to it since birth, and he strongly doubted that it was possible for it to be reconciled with the nature of a religious order.

Arrogance, a taste for luxury and ostentation, contempt for human life, a predisposition to the aggression and violence that were exalted signs of the knight's greatest virtue, courage — these were the hallmarks of the warrior aristocracy. An ethos of war as the activity of the dominant group, the "blood of the highest value," led them to exalt combat for its own sake. While his contemporaries celebrated in lyric poetry the adultery committed by young knights with the wives of their older feudal lords, the troubadour Bertrand de Born sang the following verses about the exploits of the Provençal knights who renewed their bloody conflicts with the first bloom of spring flowers:

> Iron clubs and swords, multicolored helmets,
> shields pierced and shattered
> we shall see at the very first clash,
> and countless vassals fighting
> while the steeds of the dead and wounded
> wander about unheeded.
> And when he joins the fray
> every man of high blood
> thinks of nothing but slicing off heads and arms:
> better dead than alive and defeated!
> I say to you that it gives me not such pleasure
> to eat, drink, or sleep
> as when I hear the cry: attack!
> from both sides and the neighing
> of riderless steeds,
> and hear them crying out: Help! Help!
> and see them falling into ditches
> humble and great together in the grass,
> and I see the dead with pennants waving
> from lances thrust through their breasts.
> Barons, who have pledged
> castles, boroughs, and cities
> rather than cease to make war on the rest

How could anyone reasonably expect that the knights of the Temple, born into that world and raised from infancy with that model of behavior, could give up that way of life?

Bernard was well aware of the crisis that was threatening the Christian states in the Holy Land, and he was considering lending his moral patronage to the birth of the new order, but he was also a stubborn man and refused to compromise his convictions. He made Hugh de Payens wait for quite some time before he finally responded to the Templar's appeals for assistance. Bernard's support would be decisive for the fortunes of the Temple, but only if he could find a common ground that would satisfy both the pope and Baldwin II without betraying the good intentions of a group of penitent knights at the Temple of Solomon.

East and West — War and Self-Denial

In the ninth century, the religious community of Cluny in Burgundy became the driving force in the substantial reform of Benedictine monasticism, which called for a return to the fundamental values of self-denial, purity, and the rejection of any form of secular pleasure. The religious intellectuals who subscribed to these values wished to bring this model of spirituality to the general populace in order to foster more Christian behavior — especially among the newly powerful groups created by the decline of the empire, whose cultural values were still dramatically similar to those of the pagan tradition in its exaltation of violence. In 930, Abbot Odo of Cluny wrote a biography of Saint

Gerald of Aurillac, a great feudal lord who had become a saint by living according to his social station in a Christian way, that is, by using his power, even military power, not to plunder and pillage but to defend the defenseless people of Christ. The biography was intended partly as propaganda; the author wished to demonstrate that even warriors on horseback (*potentes*) could serve God if they respected divine law and abstained from unjustified violence. While the model proposed by Abbot Odo still resembled the ascetic figure of the monk, since Saint Gerald had embraced chastity and nurtured that contempt for the world so typical of the spirit of reformed monasticism, the Clunian commitment to Christianizing the lifestyle of the military elite persisted. One hundred years later, Cluny produced the biography of another warrior-saint who had achieved sainthood by living a life more typical for a man of his class. Saint Bouchard, count of Vendôme, had entered a monastery as an older man after leading a laudable life as a just feudal lord, faithful husband, and loyal servant of King Hugh Capet.

The reformed spirituality of Cluny gave rise to the new monastic ideal of Cîteaux, which Bernard had embraced, enriching it with his mysticism and his fervent preaching. Cistercian monasticism had inherited from Cluny the commitment to promoting greater Christianization of secular customs — one Bernard had fulfilled in part by convincing some of his own relatives and other men of the aristocratic class, such as the count of Champagne, to embrace the life of the cloister.

The Augustinian priests who had welcomed Hugh de Payens and his comrades in Jerusalem had a religious outlook that was radically different in certain respects from that of Peter Damian and many monastic orders in the West. For the Augustinians, religion meant first and foremost service to others, especially to the downtrodden; it was understood in the context of a daily battle against evil in the world using the arms of the faith. Saint Augustine had praised the actions of those who dedicated their lives to the defense of the oppressed as a just war, waged in the name of the supreme good of peace, and his argument was clothed in military imagery. Deeply rooted in the culture of the East, the model of the religious combatant was painted in a mystic light. Leaving aside the controversial and unresolved question of whether or not the Templars were influenced by the *ribat*, or the Islamic idea of holy war, it must be noted that the Bible contained many examples of men sanctified for the defense of their faith: among them, King David, leader of his people and God's chosen one; and Gideon, also chosen by God to lead his soldiers to victory. The figure of the religious warrior, abundantly exalted in the Old Testament, was successfully repurposed by the militant spirituality of the Augustinians as a way of ensuring salvation for the poor and underprivileged. When Payens and his knights presented themselves to the priests of the Holy Sepulchre with their offer to defend Christian pilgrims, the Augustinians had no difficulty in seeing the goodness and justness of this proposal. Given the embattled state of the Holy Land, these knights, defenders of the defenseless, were taking upon themselves a just mission, serving God with their arms to obtain remission of their sins.

If such a model had been proposed in the same terms in the West, where ecclesiastic culture viewed the practice of war with suspicion, especially in light of the continuing violence that bands of wayward knights perpetrated against the defenseless, the nascent Templar brotherhood would have been condemned immediately. Perhaps that is why Bernard, when first approached by Hugh de Payens and probably (though not certainly) having received the letter from the king of Jerusalem, asking him to perform the absurd task of writing a monastic rule "not discordant with the clamors of war," decided at first to respond with eloquent silence. Payens's sojourn in Europe, his discussions with influential members of the political and religious elite, including the pope, and his repeated attempts to explain his endeavor to Bernard himself probably helped Western society develop a more realistic view of the conditions of life in the Holy Land. Reflecting at length on Baldwin II's request, Bernard realized that the spiritual model of the knights of the Temple was not in contradiction to his convictions. Indeed, it offered knights a way to escape the violence and perdition of secular life because it bound them to take up arms only for the defense of a just cause, thus helping shape the life and thought of the social elite to become more Christian. This was the same goal toward which reformed monasticism had been actively working for two centuries.

The key lay in the penitential intentions of the knights of the Temple and in the purely defensive aims that characterized the early days of Hugh de Payens's brotherhood. Those who became Templars wished to atone for their sins by risking their lives to defend the Holy Land. It was a lifelong crusade, and if they died, their souls would be those of men who fell in service to the church and the faith. Killing Saracens meant murdering murderers, eliminating those who had made themselves the instruments of evil: this was not homicide but *malicide*, the killing of evil. As Saint Michael the Archangel, leader of the celestial forces against the powers of darkness, defeats the devil in the great battle of the last day, so does the Templar knight serve the faith by defeating its enemies. And isn't the Virgin Mary herself, to whom Bernard was devoted, the one who crushes under her foot the head of the serpent, the incarnation of evil?

The ethic of war would lend itself to an honorable cause, but the order would not survive if it lost sight of its original values of penitence and spiritual poverty. The innate arrogance of knighthood would need to be tempered by the inflexible practice of personal humility, so the spirit of service would always come before material objectives and the cause would always come before the individual. The Temple would require the most severe discipline, harsh enough to crush the pride and desire for self-aggrandizement characteristic of the military aristocracy. If knights wished to be Templars, they would have to subject themselves to a regime of absolute obedience, renouncing their free will to submit themselves completely to the will of their superiors.

In this way a strongly homogenous and cohesive body would be born, an organization that could function admirably as long as its commanders maintained strict surveillance and inflexible discipline. The Order of the Knights Templar could become a model of perfection in Christian society, but its leaders had to assume and exercise great moral responsibility toward the church, which had accepted them within its ranks. If they were up to bearing this burden, Bernard was willing to give his assent and offer to the Templar cause his extraordinary spiritual and intellectual gifts.

The Power of an Ideal

In January 1129, at the Council of Troyes, Pope Honorius II's envoy Cardinal Matthew of Albano officially recognized the Order of the Knights Templar. Bernard made his authority felt at the council. In addition to the elderly founder of the Citeaux community, Stephen Harding, and other leading members of the Cistercian order, there were a significant number of people present who shared Bernard's spiritual and political persuasions. The abbot of Clairvaux had organized what amounted to a network of consensus at Troyes.

At the council, Hugh de Payens outlined the customs followed by the brotherhood up to that time, so that the council fathers could evaluate them and decide which should be discarded and which maintained in the new rule that would govern the life of the new religious order. After long discussions, not without some discord, the council agreed on a religious model that would thoroughly address the needs of the Holy Land: an ethics and a way of life suited to the necessities of war but not contrary to the dignity of a religious order.

As expressly declared in the prologue to the text approved by the Council of Troyes, Bernard wrote the Templar rule, which was modeled on the Benedictine rule but incorporated the Templars' original code of ethics. This code was based on the Eastern spirituality of the Augustinian clergy who offered them hospitality and provided their basic religious training as well as their liturgy — the liturgy of the Holy Sepulchre, which the Temple would continue to follow to its very end. But there is no doubt that Bernard's vision of asceticism is the foundation of the rule practiced by this unusual religious brotherhood, with its dual vocation of battling physical enemies as well as spiritual ones.

*   *   *

At the beginning of 1130, Pope Honorius II came down with a serious illness, and Chancellor Aymeric, in agreement with the Frangipani family, took him to the monastery of Saint Gregory in order to protect him from the Pierleonis. Honorius died during the night of February 13–14. His supporters elected as his successor the Roman Gregorio Papareschi, who took the name of Innocent II (1130–43). As a cardinal, he had negotiated the 1122 Concordat of Worms, which had put an end to the conflict between the pope and the Holy Roman emperor over the investiture of bishops.

The Pierleoni family, sensing that their adversaries were weak, quickly organized an attack. An assembly of cardinals loyal to the Pierleonis proclaimed the election of Innocent II illegitimate and elected instead Pietro Pierleoni, or Anaclete II, creating a schism in the church. Innocent II was forced to flee Rome for Burgundy, where he sought protection from the friends of Chancellor Aymeric. Bernard was on the front lines in the battle to defend the legitimacy of Innocent II's election to the papacy, and he worked ceaselessly to gain the support of the sovereigns of France and England, the Holy Roman emperor, and the bishops of a number of important northern Italian cities.

In 1135, at the Council of Pisa, which marked an important victory for Innocent II, the pope ratified the rule of the Templars. It is probable that Innocent himself completed it by adding a list of religious holidays that the brothers of the Temple were required to observe with special solemnity. From around 1135–37, Bernard composed a warmly enthusiastic treatise entitled *In Praise of the New Knighthood*, which delineated the model of the holy warrior in the figure of the ideal Templar knight.

In 1138, on the death of the antipope Anaclete II, the battle of Innocent II to regain the papal throne came to a happy conclusion, thanks in no small part to the work of Bernard, who lent the cause his moral authority and his exceptional powers of persuasion. The antipope Victor IV, successor to Anaclete II, officially recognized the illegitimacy of his own position and swore allegiance to Innocent II, who was finally able to return to Rome.

In 1139, Innocent II issued the papal bull *Omne datum optimum* (*Every Perfect Gift*), which set forth the essential conditions for the growth of the Order of the Knights Templar. In recognition of the blood offered for the defense of the Christian faith, the papal decree granted the Templars complete independence from ecclesiastical and secular authorities, freeing them from obedience to the patriarch of Jerusalem and making them accountable only to the pope. The grand master and the general chapter of the order would be able to manage its life and customs without any interference, except from the pope. To ensure that this independence became a concrete reality, the Templars were given the right to have their own priests, exempt from the control of bishops and archbishops. The dictum also contained concessions of an economic nature. It was amended and further enriched by subsequent papal bulls, namely *Milites Templi* (*Soldiers of the Temple*) and *Militia Dei* (*Soldiers of God*), which rendered the Temple exempt from taxes, so that all of its resources could be dedicated to its commitment to the Holy Land. They also protected its complete independence from secular and church powers, preventing sovereigns, feudal lords, or bishops from pressing the Templars into service for special interests of their own.

Every Perfect Gift, requested and obtained by Bernard from his former student Innocent II at a moment when the victorious pontiff was not in a position to deny anything to his former teacher, completed Bernard's own *In Praise of the New Knighthood*. The papal decree granted the Templars extraordinary political and economic privileges that all but ensured the order's success. Within a few short years, Payens and his knights had a network of buildings (Templar houses) so vast as to render necessary the division of the order into provinces, each directed by its own provincial master. European society acclaimed the heroism of the Templars, supporting their cause with new vocations and donations. Many nobles who continued to live their lives in the secular world asked to be spiritually affiliated with the order, which gladly welcomed them.

The Benedictine theologian Guibert of Nogent, one

of the most renowned thinkers of the time, asserted that if God had divided society into three fundamental orders, entrusting to one the mission to pray for all (the religious), to another to work for all (peasants and artisans), and to the last to fight to defend the first two (the nobility), a true earthly and spiritual perfection was realized in the new knights of the Temple, in that they united in themselves the mission of the two higher classes (the religious and the nobility), becoming in a sense the very pillars of the world.

In the warrior-brothers of the Temple the meekness and humility of the true monk were united with the courage and noble intent of the virtuous knight. There are many theories regarding the mysterious meaning of the Templar seal showing two knights astride the same horse. The most credible refers to the double character of the Templars, which brings together the material skills of the warrior and the spiritual gifts of the monk. The Templar knight represented the perfect achievement of that ideal combination of physical force and inner strength so exalted in the twelfth-century epic poem *The Song of Roland*, which celebrated Roland and Oliver, brothers in arms and heroes of a great battle against the Saracen enemy:

> Roland is strong and Oliver is wise:
> Both are extraordinarily brave:
> Once they are both on their horses in arms,
> Not even at the cost of death will they flee from battle
> Valorous are the counts and elevated their words
> As the pagan felons rabidly advance

Bernard was too intelligent and practical to think that all Templars would successfully embody the ideal that grew out of his mystic vision of the world and of man, but what was most important to him was to give them a model, a mirror of behavior and an ethical horizon they could always keep in mind and reflect on with regret each time they fell into error.

Monks in Arms?

Was the Temple a monastic order in the strict sense of the term? Templars were not ordained and never became priests, unlike members of other religious orders. Although the Templars took the three vows of poverty, obedience, and chastity, access to the ministry of the priesthood — which conferred the power to administer the sacraments — was not possible. A special canonical interdiction prohibited priests from engaging in combat or spilling blood. In *Every Perfect Gift*, Pope Innocent II laid the legal groundwork for the order to have its own chaplains. These chaplains, however, were priests who had been ordained prior to joining the brotherhood, and it was absolutely prohibited to deploy them on combat missions.

By the early 1300s, the number of Templar chaplains had dwindled to such an extent that they were no longer present in all the houses. At that time, priests who belonged to other orders rode around to various Templar houses in an area to guarantee the brothers a minimum level of religious service. According to their original rule, the Templars had to follow a regime of prayer of nine liturgical hours that spanned the entire day, so it is quite likely that their monastic life had deteriorated over the years. Nonetheless, the Temple was still considered a religious order in every respect. As Bernard observed, "It is therefore something worthy of admiration and exceedingly singular to see how they are as meek as lambs and, at the same time, more ferocious than lions, so that I almost doubt whether it would be better to refer them in both ways, in so far as they lack neither the meekness of the monk nor the courage of the warrior."

III

The Templar Code of Honor

The Nobility of the Chivalric Code

Bernard recognized that the Templar ideal represented a new way of life for men belonging to the ranks of knighthood, and he referred to this ideal constantly throughout his treatise, "I mean to allude to a new kind of knight, absolutely unknown in previous eras, who devotes all of his energies to the struggle on both fronts, against flesh and blood and against the evil spirits in the air." For practical reasons, Templars were recruited from the ranks of the military aristocracy. There was no intention to exclude the other social classes, but what was needed to defend the Holy Land were knights. There was also an important corollary, which Bernard probably saw as an advantage in the process of training new recruits: as knights, therefore as soldiers, candidates for admission to the Temple would already have received in their secular lives the necessary instruction in certain values that would prove very useful to the new order.

When Bernard and the senior clergy present at Troyes designed the Templar model, it was with one fundamental realization: this new religious order could not be founded on the customs observed in monastic environments, which demanded the renunciation of the world and mortification of the flesh. On the contrary, Templars were expected to be fully engaged with the world because the order had been created explicitly to defend the Kingdom of Jerusalem, and this special vocation required them to maintain a close and continuous relationship with the king and to collaborate with him on the development of political strategies. Their participation in military activity also prevented them from fasting regularly or performing other forms of penitence such as wearing a sackcloth, a practice that would weaken them physically. Indeed, their constant training, indispensable for keeping them battle-ready, inevitably made their lives within the monastery very much like a continuation of their lives in the world.

Bernard was the guiding spirit among the council fathers in this work of great pragmatism. Since what was needed in the Holy Land was a religious knighthood, the authors of the Templar rule made a careful study of the characteristics of the lay knighthood and tried to identify, among its many often violent and negative aspects, those meritorious qualities that lent themselves well to being governed by Christian morality. Once identified, these were emphasized and promoted by appropriate doctrine and cultivated by establishing a rigorous regimen of discipline that made those virtues into the pillars of a new and sophisticated code of conduct.

They recognized four cardinal points of the aristocratic military ethic that coincided with the Templar model:
physical strength; courage with honor; loyalty to the group;
and the spirit of sacrifice. These four knightly virtues were
associated with corresponding Christian values, and formed
the conceptual framework that would make the Templars
into ideal knights — elevated further by their religious vocation. The result was a way of life that was both extremely
noble and extremely challenging, and, as conceived by
Bernard, seemingly elitist: it was suited only to a few, a select minority of knights able to combine the right physical
and psychological qualities with a very strong religious
commitment.

Marks of Humility, Marks of Excellence

The biggest stumbling block on the path to this new religious knighthood was pride — an attitude long encouraged
and reinforced within the military aristocracy. The challenge was to reconcile the monastic identity and vocation
with a quality that Christian tradition considered a mortal
sin — and one that proved to be a strong incentive to
demonstrating valor and exceptional skill in combat. The
solution to this conundrum lay in a compromise: a Templar had to maintain the utmost humility as an individual
while feeling intense pride in belonging to the Temple.

To earn and nurture people's respect and admiration,

Templars subjected themselves to inflexible discipline in all circumstances, even in times of peace. Brothers who were sent out among the laity to perform some task had to live irreproachably. The rule expressly required them to be a visible example of holiness and moderation, so Templars had to observe all the precepts to which they were bound and endeavor to make an excellent impression on everyone they met.

Templars were obliged to pay particular attention to their outward appearance and maintain order and cleanliness, while they aspired to the frugality that was supposed to distinguish their behavior in every way. The description provided by Bernard in his treatise is eloquent:

> They shave their hair, convinced of the words of the Apostle that it is shameful for a man to have long hair. Never affected, rarely washed, rather they present themselves with their hair disheveled or bristly, dirty with dust, their skin dark from their armor and the rays of the sun.

Striking as it is, this image was probably exaggerated to emphasize the sobriety of Templar life compared to the excessive frivolity of lay knights, whom Bernard ridiculed as a bunch of effeminates devoted to luxury:

> You dress your horses in silk and over your armor you wear all kinds of fluttering veils; you paint your lances, shields, and saddles, and decorate your reins and spurs with gold, silver, or precious stones. . . . Like women, you cultivate a

mane that becomes an obstacle to your vision; you hinder your stride with long, vaporous tunics; you bury your delicate and tender hands in ample, enfolding sleeves.

The council-approved rule determined that the Templars' appearance must be inspired by a principle of just measure, dignity, and decorum so as not to provoke the criticism of the malicious. Internal and external cleanliness was indispensable for those who serve God, in accordance with the divine precept, "You shall be clean because I am clean." The custom of keeping hair, beards, and mustaches cut short was explicitly dictated by personal decorum but also as a condemnation of secular fashion. In accordance with the original spirit of poverty promoted by founder Hugh de Payens, fabrics used for Templar clothing were of poor quality: a very humble linen cloth for sergeants, a slightly better one for knights. Each possessed several items of clothing, which ensured a good level of hygiene compared to the standards of the time, two sets of undergarments to allow for a change during washing, and a towel reserved for drying the head, which evidently was not completely shaven, plus a tablecloth.

The rule absolutely banned hosiery with raised points of the kind that was very much in fashion among lay knights, as well as long gowns, which lent the figure greater stature and dignity. Templar dress had to be the proper length: short enough so as not to hinder the knight's freedom of movement in combat, but long enough so as not to expose the brothers to ridicule by leaving their legs excessively bare. Fur coats were not allowed, except for ram or sheepskin, and cloaks were supplied in two versions, one lined with feathers for cold weather.

All the clothes and accessories that the Templars owned prior to taking their vows were deposited with the draper, who was obliged, however, to refuse the most valuable garments, such as those made of multicolored fabrics or dyed scarlet. New brothers' secular clothes were donated to the poor or given to their sergeants, which could be further evidence of the latter's less than total integration into the Templar brotherhood, at least in the early decades of the order. The draper was also charged with inspecting the clothes of all the brethren and ordering those in violation of the rule to make amends.

Each Templar was given a straw mattress, a sheet, and a blanket, which could be replaced by a quilt stuffed with wool or rough linen velvet. Although community living and the heat of Palestine made it absolutely necessary for the brothers to avoid the spread of parasites, they were prohibited from taking baths without permission from their commander. This was probably based on the belief that indiscriminate bathing led to health risks or physical weakness. Indeed, the prohibition was one in a long list that included the practice of being bled, taking medicine, spending time in town without purpose, and spurring one's horse to breakaway speed. Another precept provided that the brothers were excused from going immediately to prayer upon hearing the sound of the bell if they were in the midst of making bread, forging iron, shoeing a horse, or washing their hair.

Arms, both the symbol and the expression of military pride, were furnished by the order and were basic and utilitarian in appearance. The embellishment of weapons with gold or silver plating, then in fashion in the secular world, was expressly prohibited. Sometimes wealthy benefactors donated splendidly decorated weapons to the Temple. In such cases these could be accepted, on condition that the precious metal plating was partially tarnished, so the brothers could not be accused of having bought them. If these were new or untarnished, the decision to accept or refuse them belonged to the grand master, who generally chose to sell them. Also prohibited were shield and lance covers, which were considered useless luxuries.

Each knight was outfitted with a hauberk, or chain-mail tunic, a chain-mail vest, chain-mail leggings, a helmet, a spear, a lance, a shield, a mace, a military cassock, a padded surplice to wear under the hauberk, and a long linen shirt to be worn over a shorter one that was an undergarment. Sergeants wore a sleeveless hauberk, iron leggings with no protection for the back of the legs, and a helmet.

In times of peace, when the brothers could remove their armor and devote their days to prayer and work (*ora et labora*) just like other monks in orders regulated by the Benedictine rule, they wore long, narrow-sleeved tunics over their standard undergarments. The tunic was cinched at the waist by a leather belt and concealed by a mantle, which covered the whole body and was outfitted with a hood. The mantle was emblazoned with a red cross, which ˌ symbolized and proclaimed their vocation to martyrdom. This privilege was bestowed on the Templars by Pope Eugene III at the Council of Paris in 1147.

A Harmonious Balance of Body and Spirit

> God chose these servants, gathering them together from the ends of the earth, from among the strongest of Israel, in order to carefully and loyally protect the bed of the true Solomon, that is, the Sepulchre, all furnished with swords and expert in the art of war.

Bernard's ideas about the organizational structure of the new Templar brotherhood were very clear. It must be a corps of select combatants, masters of the military profession with the necessary experience that would make them immediately useful to the cause for which the Temple had been created.

The practice of admitting young boys, tolerated by the Benedictine rule, was prohibited. The order could not take upon itself the expense necessary to maintain such future Templars until they were mature enough to fight effectively; besides, the presence of adolescents within Templar houses would have been a source of disciplinary problems.

How could young boys be prevented from engaging in scurrilous practical jokes, games, provocations, fighting, and attempts to flee the house in pursuit of romantic adventures? The Templar rule also expressly recognized that youngsters who made such a choice at an immature age were at great risk of changing their minds and abandoning the order, which could potentially cause scandal and serious damage to the moral image of the Temple.

The lifestyle outlined in the Templar rule was highly challenging. For the order to be successful, the candidate must feel a profound desire to detach himself from the world and undergo personal purification, just as Payens and his comrades had been inspired to take the vows in Jerusalem by their desire to atone for their sins through a life of sacrifice. Such a choice was well suited to grown men, already expert in secular life and possibly disgusted by its vanities, who were ready for the total conversion that made the order worthy of being called monastic. The ideal Templar knight, in the eyes of Bernard, was a mature widower who could leave the management of his possessions to his firstborn son, so that he could dedicate the rest of his life to the religious knighthood — akin to the model of Hugh de Payens.

But unlike other monks, the Templars could not allow themselves to mortify their own flesh, which meant beating or whipping oneself or wearing a hairshirt, as a form of penance. Neither could they follow other monks' hygienic, dietary, and psychological practices — such as fasting, abstaining from certain foods, and other forms of self-denial — that might help them remain faithful to their vows. They had to take care of their bodies and ensure that they were healthy, efficient, and properly trained for combat. The consumption of meat and wine helped them stave off the physical weakness that could have been an ally in the struggle to remain sexually abstinent.

The recruitment of mature men, still able in war but no longer youthful, would make the obligation to chastity more attainable and limit the possibility of Templars leaving the house and allowing themselves to be found in compromising situations. In order to strengthen their resolve, single knights were carefully prevented from having contact with married knights in temporary service to the Temple, who were required to sleep in separate quarters. The presence of these volunteer soldiers who had not undergone monastic conversion and who had not taken the religious vows could have created a barracks atmosphere, with vulgar exchanges and derisive behavior, that would have been detrimental to the Templars. For similar reasons, it was prohibited to fraternize with women and for Templars to kiss even their closest female relatives.

Bernard and the council fathers probably had few illusions that all the brothers would be faithful to their vow of chastity, a promise that required great sacrifice and was alien to the mentality of the military aristocracy. The image of women as objects of conquest mirrored the violence reserved by the ruling classes for their social inferiors, as told in ballads of the encounter between a knight and a shepherdess, a case in which even the refined treatise by Andreas Capellanus, *The Art of Courtly Love*, recommended the use of force. Even in the most rarified expressions of epic and courtier poetry, the sexual objectification of women was all too legible.

The rule provided that if a brother allowed himself to be tempted by a prostitute, he was not to reveal it to his brethren, so as not to create a precedent and occasion for sinful thoughts. If a brother was discovered on the premises of a brothel and caused public scandal, he lost his status as a Templar. As late as the beginning of the fourteenth century, during the initiation ceremony, some preceptors instructed the new Templar to abstain from keeping the company of women, but if he could not refrain, he had to ensure that no one found out about it.

Further evidence of such pragmatism was provided in the drafting of the measures governing the practice of hunting and jousting tournaments, the favorite pastimes of lay knights. It is commonly believed that these were absolutely prohibited for Templars, but that is not quite accurate. Obliging a knight to renounce completely what had been the most prestigious and enjoyable activities of his secular life would certainly result in numerous violations and greater difficulties among novices adapting to their new lives. Bernard and the council fathers agreed on a compromise that greatly limited the practice of these "vices" to very specific conditions.

The rule expressly prohibited falconry, labeling it a "worldly amusement," and the decorum, modesty, and seriousness that the Templars, as monks, were held to maintain were judged incompatible with the rowdy and violently roguish behavior typical of the hunt:

> We condemn in common accord the custom of hunting birds with other birds. Indeed, such profane amusements are ill suited to the monastic condition. Rather, brothers should listen to religious teachings, participate in prayer sessions, and each day with tears in their eyes confess their sins to God. For this reason no professed Templar shall accompany laity who practice hunting with falcons or other birds of prey. Since it is every monk's duty to behave with decency and modesty, without abandoning himself to merriment, to speak little and with measured tones only about opportune subjects, we prohibit all brothers from going into the woods to hunt with a bow or to go there with those who do so unless it is to protect them from attack by Saracens; and in any case, a Templar dare not shout incitements or make the noises typical of the hunt with hounds, or spur his horse to the frenetic pursuit of some animal.

Rather than prohibit hunting altogether, the rule allowed Templars to accompany those on a hunt, in order to protect them from Saracen attack, an entirely plausible situation in the context of the Holy Land, which was under constant threat of aggression from neighboring Muslim states. This innocent pretext could be raised by any Templar at any time without risk of contradiction, and it ensured brothers with a passion for the hunt the possibility of always taking part, albeit in a subdued fashion. If, however, the hunt was aimed at eliminating the lions that infested the Christian territories of Palestine, all prohibitions were removed and Templars were free to participate actively and use weapons.

The Templar rule made no explicit reference to tournaments, and not even Bernard included it in his list of prohibited amusements:

> They detest chess and games of chance and are horrified by the hunt. Nor do they amuse themselves, as is the custom, in fowling. They disdain and abhor as vanities and deceptive folly actors, soothsayers, storytellers, obscene songs, and theatrical performances.

Although in his treatise *In Praise of the New Knighthood* Bernard had condemned the ostentatious violence and luxury typical of jousting tournaments, they nevertheless provided useful opportunities for training in peacetime.

The demands of combat ruled out the outright condemnation of passionate outbursts, impulsive conduct, or other manifestations of vitality and strength. While it was right to demand great discipline from the Templars, such behaviors could not be totally repressed at the risk of encouraging the brothers to adopt an asceticism that would weaken them and undermine their readiness for battle. The king of Jerusalem had been quite explicit in his letter to the abbot of Clairvaux: "Devise for the brothers such customs and habits of life that will not be in contrast with the clamor and harshness of war, but which show themselves to be useful for Christian principles."

A strong tendency toward asceticism existed among twelfth-century Templars and was more prevalent than previously believed. The rule actually had to prohibit brothers who were ill from getting up for the recital of matins, or early morning prayers, and from fasting beyond special liturgical occasions, and required them to eat in pairs so they could supervise one another and report those who fasted without permission.

Another precept stated rather curiously:

A witness worthy of the highest trust has told us that you listen to the divine office of the Mass while remaining standing the whole time, without observing the just measure. We feel obliged to condemn this custom. After the psalm, "Come let us exalt in the Lord," you are all to sit during the antiphon and the hymn, whether you are healthy or sick, so as not to give cause for scandal. And we are all agreed in ordering that you pray observing the just measure in body and spirit, that is, sitting and standing when provided and with simplicity, in utmost reverence and without shouting so that each does not disturb the other.

What possible scandal could be caused by the sight of Templars praying on their feet even when they could sit? And why was it necessary to instruct them to moderate the volume with which they lifted their voices in prayer? It is probable that the drafters of the rule wished to temper the level of the brothers' enthusiasm, which, if left uncontrolled, might have resulted in fanaticism. The law of moderation, Bernard's governing principle, was applied to reign in the intense religious fervor among the Templars described by Ernoul the Frank in his chronicle of Jerusalem.

To Live and Die under a Flag

Contempt for your own life, or the capacity to make no effort to save yourself in battle, was an extremely useful quality in the context of the Christian states in the Holy Land. Courage was a required resource for all combatants, and it was worthy of praise, even while attempting to reconcile the values of the chivalric code with the Templars' religious vows. For the Templars, audacity, the prime virtue of the knight in *The Song of Roland*, must be balanced by wisdom — understood not only as sagacity in making the best use of one's resources but also as moderation and harmony among fellow warriors. Belonging to an elite military and social group came with the duty to defend its moral image. The group could not afford to debase its preeminence with behavior that deviated from the code that distinguished it.

An Arab chronicler of the time, Emir Usāma ibn Munqidh, provides this portrait of the nobility of the Holy Land:

> Among the Franks — may God send them to their ruin! — there is no human virtue that they appreciate more than valor, and no one has prominence of high rank except the knights, the only persons among them with valor. It is they who give counsel, judge, and command. . . .
>
> Once the knights have established the sentence, neither the king nor any other leader can modify or undo it, so great is the knight amongst them. The king told me on that occasion: "O you, on my valor, yesterday I was so glad!" "That God should make you glad, Your Majesty," I replied, "what were you so glad about?" "They told me you were a great knight, and I didn't believe you were a knight." "Majesty," I replied, "I am a knight of my race and my people." When a knight is tall and slender, the more they admire him.

The Temple was composed primarily of knights. It was not a question of social class that induced Bernard and the council fathers to close the ranks of the Temple but rather the awareness that such a model of life required long and progressive training and could not be learned on command. The Templar model was especially designed for this caste, which, in the military reality of the early twelfth century, was the determining factor in the fighting strength of any army:

> Whoever you are, knight of Christ, you who have made such a lofty religious choice, in order to keep faith with your vows you will have to give proof of your great will and firmness. And if you succeed, with purity and perseverance, you will have merited your place among the martyrs who gave their lives in the name of Christ. In this order chivalry is reborn and flourishes, that which by disdaining justice betrayed its task of defending the poor and the churches and turned to the cruelty of looting, pillaging, and murder. . . .
>
> We hereby order that their clothing be always of just one color, either black or white, and of the poorest fabric. To all those knights who have embraced the Templar profession we grant, wherever possible, the right to wear white clothes in both winter and summer, so that they may be recognized as having abandoned the life of darkness to reconcile themselves with their Creator through a pure and immaculate life. White indicates perfect chastity, and chastity means salvation for the intellect and health for the body. If any knight fails to maintain his chastity he will not go to his eternal rest and see God, in accordance with St. Paul who said, "Let us seek peace with all and chastity, without which nobody shall see God."

Those who did not come from the ranks of the military aristocracy were welcome and were provided for in the rule approved at Troyes, but at that time such recruits, who were called sergeants, probably did not participate fully in the Templar brotherhood. There is some evidence that the condition of the sergeants, at least in the early days of the order, was considered inferior even on the ethical and religious level:

> We are in accord in decidedly condemning and prohibiting a practice that was widely shared among the Templars: even the sergeants and servants wore white clothing, a fact which produced considerable damage. Indeed, in the regions beyond the mountains there appeared false Templars, married brethren, and other individuals who passed themselves off as Templars while they still belonged to the world. These people and their behavior brought shame upon the order, and filled with false pride those who were in service to the Temple only temporarily. From now on, they should have only black clothes, and if they do not find them, they should wear clothes available locally, which should be of just one color and of the poorest fabric.

According to Antonio Sicci da Vercelli, who had worked for the Templars for forty years and knew their archives well because he had used them for administrative purposes, initially the brotherhood had been reserved for knights only, while the sergeants were relegated to a lesser role and were for the most part paid for their services. Only later did the order decide to grant sergeants full membership in the Temple. Further confirmation of the separate roles of knights and sergeants was provided by the different colors of their clothes, imposed by Bernard, who was inspired by the habits of Cluny and Citeaux. In those two orders, white robes were reserved for monks, while lay brothers dressed in brown.

The martial excellence of the knights had to be made manifest in battle. The prestigious Templar banner of white and black, about whose symbolic significance historians are still uncertain, was the visible representation of the order's religious and military pride. The Templars were called upon to make the ultimate sacrifice, to lay down their lives in defense of the Holy Land. The only refuge was the solidarity of other Templars ready to risk their lives to save a fellow warrior. The rule commanded:

> No one must leave his position without the permission of his commander, not even if he is wounded; and if he finds himself unable to request leave, he must send a comrade to do it for him. And if by chance it should happen that the Christians are defeated — God save us! — no brother must leave the field of battle as long as the banner of the Temple is still flying, and anyone in violation will be expelled forever from the order. When a brother sees that the Templar banner has fallen, he must go to the first banner of the Hospitallers or other Christian combatants that he is able to find; and if they too should go down in defeat, then he shall be free to save himself as God may advise him to do.

The precepts of the rule were certainly not followed to the letter by all members of the order, and it would be naive to assume that there were no cases of cowardice or desertion. Nevertheless, during the twelfth century the Temple was a compact and cohesive corps, characterized by iron discipline.

The Sacred Bond of Solidarity

The Templar organization was highly efficient and decidedly innovative for its time. According to the military historian Claude Gaier, "The new knighthood of the Temple, expert and organized, and endowed with its own ideology, prefigured those qualities that would constitute the superiority of recent armies over those of the Middle Ages and the ancien regime in general. . . . The Temple was incontestably the best that the classic Middle Ages was able to produce in terms of military discipline."

The rule had been designed to maximize internal cohesion, esprit de corps, and coordinated action in an age in which tactics were still strongly based on individual valor. Characterized by a remarkable unity, the Temple was the only part of the crusading army capable of maintaining constant discipline. While crossing the mountains of Anatolia during the second crusade, King Louis VII of France witnessed the disruptive conduct of the Christian contingent; the Templars were the only division that exhibited order.

All hailing from the social milieu of the lay knighthood, the knights of the Temple shared a system of values and a set of behaviors that were conducive to cohesion even before their induction into the order. However, many characteristic behaviors had to be moderated, disciplined, and reconciled with Christian morality.

The impulse to distinguish oneself, inherent in the cavalier mentality, was punished. No Templar was authorized to modify his uniform. Whoever tried to improve his personal accessories, believing them unworthy, would be outfitted with accessories of even lower quality. This emphasis on the uniform served to reinforce the community, to the interest of which each Templar must always, and in all ways, subject himself, erasing all traces of his own individuality in deference to the group.

This sense of community was exalted and identified with the Christian concept of brotherhood. Every Templar had the duty to watch over his comrades, and if he noticed some shortcoming he was to exhort the guilty party, with the utmost discretion, to redeem himself before being discovered by his superiors so as to help him avoid punishment. If his appeal was not heeded, he was to turn to another of his brethren to ask, again with the utmost circumspection, that he convince their brother to repent. Only if this attempt failed was he was obliged to inform his commander.

Any form of behavior that might undermine the cohesion of the group — and there were frequent episodes of pride, envy, jealousy, backbiting, gossip, and slander — was categorically condemned. Brothers were strictly forbidden from claiming the horse or the furnishings of another as their own, and if their own furnishings were inadequate to their needs, they were required to go to their commander and request replacements. Even the practice of trading equipment among brothers was censured. Everything belonged to the Temple, and such private arrangements were stigmatized as attempts to carve out niches of insidious individualism within the community. Gift-giving, however, was freely allowed as long as the gift was modest, such as a used garment, so as not to contravene the principle of poverty.

The prohibition against keeping containers with latches and locks, which seemed superfluous since brothers were forbidden to possess any personal objects worth more than a nominal sum, other than their basic furnishings and accessories, was probably meant to discourage the concept of personal property. For similar reasons, Templars could not read in private the letters sent to them by their relatives, nor accept gifts from them without the approval of their superiors.

Most of the provisions governing behavior during battle were aimed at inhibiting individualism, which probably had characterized the knights' behavior during their military experiences in secular life. Templar precepts forbade the brothers to break formation, deviate from the rules of engagement established by their superiors, advance ahead of others, or take any action on their own initiative. The only exception: saving the life of a Christian or a fellow Templar.

The bond of community solidarity extended to all Templars who were no longer able to participate in military operations: the elderly and the sick. Respect for the elderly was associated with the concept of charity to the weak. Caring for the infirm was an obligation that the Templar rule derived directly from the Gospels, and the numerous provisions concerning the duties of brothers as caregivers demonstrate that it was regularly fulfilled.

The commemoration of deceased brothers was carried out with a solemnity in keeping with the Templar's awareness that death played an inherent role in the special mission of the order. The numerous prayers for the souls of the departed were also extended to the laity who had served the Temple for a period of time without becoming permanent members, as well as the families of the brothers and all the benefactors who supported the order with material gifts and, above all, with the favor of their esteem.

Regulations and Hierarchy

The religious and administrative life of the order was governed by about seventy provisions in the Templar rule, written originally in Latin in 1129 and later, probably in the early 1200s, translated into French. Over time, the rule incorporated additional provisions that regulated various activities of the order, from liturgical practices to military service. The first addendum to the rule was a list of religious feasts the Templars were required to celebrate with special rituals and fasting. In 1163, the hierarchical statutes, the body of regulations that established the organizational hierarchy of the order, were formalized.

The Templar hierarchy was headed by the master (toward the end of the thirteenth century the title was changed to grand master to distinguish him from the provincial masters), the undisputed leader who controlled the members and the estates of the order. The statutes left no room for doubt regarding his authority: "Every precept contemplated in this rule is subject to the discretion and judgment of the master" (article 73).

Selected through a long and complex election procedure, the master of the Temple had to have the necessary experience to govern a multinational organization that was simultaneously an army, a financial enterprise for the crusades, and a diplomatic corps. Men who were experts on the Holy Land and were able to speak the languages of the countries where the order was most widely represented were preferred. On the most important questions affecting the order, the master was obliged to consult his *couvent*, a council whose advice had to be given due consideration. *Couvent* comes from the Latin *conventum*, which simply means "meeting." The rule uses this term in several different contexts, at times giving the impression that the *couvent* was comprised of all members of the order, but other sections of the rule make it clear that it referred to a council or assembly, whose size depended on the matter to be discussed.

There was a plenary meeting of all members when Templars attended a religious ceremony or deployed into battle, but there were meetings involving only the highest-ranking members when it was necessary to decide matters of vital importance. Article 98 provided that all brothers of the Temple had to obey the master, while he was held to obey his *couvent*. The word must necessarily refer to the master's council or cabinet, and cannot refer to all Templars because no organization, least of all a military corps, could manage to function if the decisions of its leader were subject to approval by all of its members.

The documentary evidence indicates that the master chose several personal advisers whom he trusted. The rule refers to them as *compagnons du mestre*, the master's companions; in the Middle Ages the word *companion* meant friend, comrade in arms, adviser. There was also a group of "ancients" or wise men, veteran Templars whom the bylaws assigned significant authority. Their approval was required for amendments or additions to the bylaws proposed by the master, and, as custodians of the Temple's history, they had to be consulted whenever a situation not covered by the bylaws called for important decisions to be made.

The master, his companions, and the ancients, along

with members of the general staff, or the order's main administrative officers, comprised the executive council of the Temple. The seneschal, or grand commander, was second in command to the grand master. He and the marshal were directly responsible for all military operations. The highest-ranking administrative officer was the commander of the Land of Jerusalem, followed by the commander of the City of Jerusalem. They were responsible for matters related to the most important strategic strongholds in the Holy Land.

Estate and asset management was the responsibility of the treasurer, an office generally held by a sergeant. In the early twelfth century, the education of the cavalier class was primarily concerned with military training, while reading and writing were considered activities more suited to clerics and merchants. At the end of the thirteenth century, the Temple's increasing involvement in banking endowed the office of treasurer with great authority, regardless of its official ranking within the hierarchy.

The new order grew quite rapidly, so Hugh de Payens's immediate successors were forced to organize the Templars' properties into provinces to ensure efficient administration. Each main province was governed by a commander, or preceptor, and divided into smaller districts (*balivie*), which in turn presided over the houses in each local area, forming an administrative network that extended throughout the Mediterranean and beyond, from Portugal to Armenia and from Scotland to the Holy Land.

All Templar commanders, from officers who oversaw provinces down to the smallest districts, convened with the general staff for the general chapter at least once a year. The chapter was held on the Feast of the Apostles and lasted several days, during which liturgical functions alternated with meetings to discuss administrative questions.

The Financial Face of the Temple

In the twelfth century the Western economy was based primarily on income from property. European nobles who wanted to give the Temple material as well as moral support donated land and buildings to the order. The records of Templar houses in France reveal remarkable growth during the twelfth century, with numerous vocations and donations, a clear sign that the religious knighthood enjoyed a reputation as a true model of moral excellence. The houses in the provinces were commercial farms as well as recruitment and training centers, where new Templars were instructed before they were sent off to the front lines in the Holy Land. The order also operated a fleet of ships to ferry its men and supplies to and from the East.

The agricultural production and the in-kind rents paid by tenants of Templar estates were converted into money and sent to the Holy Land. To facilitate this transfer, the order quickly developed sophisticated banking and financial systems, probably drawing on the experience of prominent merchants, and its ships were regular visitors to the ports of the Mediterranean. In 1179 the church issued a severe condemnation of the practice of moneylending, which was often identified with usury, but the economic times were evolving toward a greater reliance on trade and increased circulation of capital. The Templars, like other religious orders and even bishops, made loans at generally moderate interest rates, and the transactions often took the form of a pledge. The debtor pledged property as collateral to secure a loan. The inventories of Templar houses document valuable pottery, silk dresses, and other costly personal items deposited as pledges.

The original spirit of the order, based on the penitential value of poverty, and the need to dedicate all of its resources to meeting the heavy costs of defending the Holy Land led to the adoption of regulations providing for the severe punishment of the personal appropriation of money and property owned by the order. The maximum amount that a Templar could hold was fixed at the laughably modest figure of four dinars, beyond which he could be accused of theft and expelled from the order. This severe rigor gave the Temple a reputation for ironclad honesty, which was further incentive for wealthy individuals and even monarchs to deposit their capital in the strongboxes of the order. The Templars not only faithfully safeguarded these deposits, they also made them bear fruit.

One episode serves as an example to illustrate both the order's rigid code of discipline and the Templars' sense of responsibility toward their creditors. In the middle of the thirteenth century, during the first expedition of King Louis IX of France to the Holy Land, the king's brother was captured by the Saracens, who demanded a huge ransom in exchange for his release. The king turned to the Templars for a loan. One of the order's ships, equipped with locked safe deposit boxes, lay at anchor in a nearby harbor. The amount requested by the king was not excessive — and there was a precedent for the loan because one of his predecessors, Louis VII, had received a loan from the Templars during the second crusade — but this situation was much more complicated.

The rule, particularly inflexible with regard to money, contained an express prohibition against lending money to anyone outside of the Temple without the explicit consent of its superiors. In a case such as this, only the master of the Temple could come to the aid of the king because the rule provided that the master could overturn any provision of the bylaws in an emergency situation. At the time of Louis VII, the master had immediately ordered the treasurer to satisfy the needs of the king, but now the order found itself in serious difficulty because the grand master, Guillaume de Sonnac, had been killed in battle.

The biggest problem was the question of legal responsibility. Since the money on the ship belonged to private individuals who had entrusted it to the Temple, opening the safe deposit boxes to give the money to the king would amount to theft. If the owners were to request their money at that moment, the Templars would find themselves insolvent, with serious damage to the moral and financial reputation of the order.

The procedure for electing a new grand master took weeks, and it was simply not possible to wait that long. The need to act quickly, the apprehension for the king's brother in enemy hands, the king's ignorance of the Templar rule, and the overly impetuous temperament of some of the knights escalated the crisis.

Brother Etienne d'Otricourt, who as commander of the Land of Jerusalem was head of the Temple pending the election of a new grand master, came into conflict with the lord of Joinville, who had advised the king to borrow the money from the Templars, flaunting an open disregard for the rules and obligations of the order. An argument broke out between the two men, with an exchange of insults. At that point, the Templar marshal, Raymond de Vichers, an astute man with outstanding diplomatic skills, devised a stratagem that allowed Louis IX to have the money without violating the rules of the Temple and without going against the express refusal of the loan by the commander, who was, though only temporarily, his superior.

The marshal reiterated to the king that the commander had expressed the dictates of their rule in a very precise manner and that there was no way that the Templars could legally satisfy him. But the brothers wouldn't be able to do anything against a possible theft perpetrated by the king, a theft that in any case could be reimbursed with the money that Louis IX had deposited in the strong-boxes of the Temple in Acre. His suggestion created a way out of the impasse, and the incident was happily resolved.

Over the course of the thirteenth century, the popes appointed the Temple as the bank charged with safeguarding and investing church money meant to finance the crusades, while the crown of France attributed to the Templar house in Paris the role of treasury of the realm. To hold the kingdom's money, an imposing fortress, the grand Tower of the Temple, was erected in what is now the Parisian quarter of the Marais, which it continued to dominate until the tower was destroyed during the French Revolution.

Politics and Diplomacy

Defending the Kingdom of Jerusalem from the Muslims in the Holy Land, whose potentates were constantly at odds with each other, meant that the Temple did not face a unified enemy. The situation required the Templars to skillfully negotiate with one adversary or another in order to build effective yet constantly shifting alliances.

When the crusaders marched on Antioch, the Egyptian Fatimids looked with great favor on the chaos that the newly arrived Franks were creating in Palestine, and planned to negotiate an agreement with the aim of reclaiming the region that had been taken from them by the Turks. The local Arab dynasties in northern Syria were

equally satisfied at the defeat of the Turks and ready to negotiate with the Europeans, who, for their part, were anx-
ious for the support of the two most powerful families, the
Banu Munqidh of Shaizar and the Banu Ammar of Tripoli.

Whenever necessary, the local Muslim potentates
were quite adept at separating politics from religion. They
didn't necessarily view war as a question of faith, as contemporary Westerners might suppose, and they were willing to make alliances with the Christians when it was in
their interest to do so, that is, when it preserved the independence of their local territories. By fomenting discord
and promoting friendships with the enemies of its enemies, the Christian kingdom managed to survive despite
its persistent problem of insufficient troops. The Templars
were often involved in these negotiations and developed
an extraordinary capacity for dialogue. Not only the popes
and European kings but even the Byzantine emperors requested the assistance of their most renowned negotiators
for delicate diplomatic missions.

Diplomacy required the capacity to understand the
psyche of foreign peoples, whose conception of the world
and human relationships differed greatly from that of
Western thought. Since war was often conducted at the
negotiating table rather than on the battlefield, the Templars acquired a very elastic mindset, which their strategic
military training and experience broadened.

The order formed cordial relationships with several
Muslim emirs, based on common economic or political in-

terests; religious discussions were carefully avoided. This friendly coexistence required the reciprocal respect of cultural differences. These political relationships would later be used by the enemies of the order to spread rumors about the Templars' possible secret conversion to Islam.

The most famous of these alliances is the one documented by the emir of Shaizar, Usāma ibn Munqidh, an intelligent and erudite man of great faith, whom the Templars allowed to pray on the sacred rock in al-Aqsa Mosque, which was in their headquarters in Jerusalem.

When I visited Jerusalem I used to go into al-Aqsa Mosque, on one side of which was a small prayer room that the Franks had turned into a church. When I used to enter al-Aqsa Mosque, where my friends the Templars had their headquarters, they would make that small prayer room available to me so I could say my prayers there. One day I went in, uttered the prayer *Allahu akbar*, and was about to continue when a Frank pounced on me, grabbed me, and turned my face toward the East, saying, "This is the way to pray." Some Templars who were there intervened immediately, taking hold of him and leading him away, as I went back to saying my prayers. But he, taking advantage of a moment's distraction, pounced on me again, turned my face again to the East, and repeated, "This is the way to pray." The Templars intervened again, led him away, and apologized to me, saying, "He's a foreigner, just arrived a few days ago from the country of the Franks, and he's never seen anyone pray except with their face turned toward the East." "I've prayed enough," I replied; and I left, stupefied by that demon, who had become so angry and agitated on seeing someone pray in the direction of the Qibla.

Another important Muslim was granted the privilege of praying on the sacred rock and could not help but be scandalized by the devotion shown by the Templars to the Virgin Mary:

> I then saw with my own eyes one of them present himself to Emir Mu'in ad-Din — may God have mercy on them — when he was in the Mosque of the Rock, and say to him: "Do you want to see God as a baby?" "Yes," he replied, and the Frank led him to an image of Mary with the little Messiah on her lap. "This," he said, "is God as a baby."

The episode is reported in Usāma's chronicle, with a quotation from the Koran to emphasize that those words are blasphemous to a Muslim: "God almighty occupies a much higher place than what the infidels believe!"

The emir was a friend of the Templars and showed sincere benevolence toward them, but he deeply disapproved of their religious convictions. They were so far from the truth of Islam, and they actually expected him to believe that God had become man as the son of the Virgin Mary!

The religious orthodoxy of the Templars — which their patron Bernard, in view of their mission as warriors, had pushed just short of Christian fanaticism — was widely recognized; the order enjoyed great authority even with regard to purely religious questions. The Templars, together with the members of the other great military order of the Hospital of Saint John, had the prestigious assignment of escorting through Jerusalem a relic of Christ's cross during the solemn liturgical ceremony in its honor. The Templars were also ascribed the capacity to distinguish true relics from false ones. On occasion, European kings asked them to consecrate objects by bringing them to the Holy Sepulchre or other sacred places. In the middle of the thirteenth century, King Louis IX asked for the Templars' advice during his search in the Byzantine Empire for the most important relics of Christ's suffering and death. The Templars were regarded as occupying the summit of the Christian model of society. Because they were nobles as well as monks, the knights of the Temple united in themselves the two classes to which God had entrusted the difficult task of guiding humanity.

IV

In Service to the Holy Land

Outremer

The Order of the Knights Templar experienced its greatest period of growth and achievement in the years between the pontificates of Pope Innocent II (1140–43) and Pope Innocent III (1189–1216), which coincided with the golden years of the Kingdom of Jerusalem. Both pontificates marked fundamental turning points in the history of the order. Innocent II laid the groundwork by issuing the extraordinary guarantee of independence in the papal bull *Every Perfect Gift*, and Innocent III intervened wisely and discreetly to resurrect the fortunes of the order after a tragic reversal had threatened its survival. The experience of the Temple in the Holy Land, which began with the vows taken by Hugh de Payens before the patriarch of Jerusalem, is the history of an unwavering commitment to the defense of the Christian presence in the East, fulfilled through armed struggle, diplomatic mediation, and political maneuvering. The great events that mark the history of the Latin kingdom of Jerusalem also define the context in which the Templar order was born and prospered, and outside of which, after the era of the crusades had ended in failure, it would be plunged into crisis.

The area occupied by the Christians in Syria and Palestine, called Outremer because of its location beyond the Mediterranean Sea, was a thin coastal strip extending from Armenia in the north to the borders of the Fatimid caliphate of Egypt in the south. By 1109, the Christian territory was divided into four large states: the Kingdom of Jerusalem, extending from Gaza to Beirut; the County of Tripoli, from Beirut to Margat; the Principality of Antioch, from Margat to Alexandria; and the County of Edessa, which stretched northeast all the way to present-day Urfa. These Latin states were governed by noble courts in much the same way as their counterparts in Europe. They were often rocked by dynastic disputes, which, together with the scarcity of available troops and the latent threat of Muslim attack, put the security of the Christian population in a constant state of uncertainty.

The most widely used language in Outremer was French, the mother tongue of most of the crusaders, but it had absorbed elements from Venetian dialect and the languages of nearby maritime cities. Genoa and Venice played a fundamental role in the political and economic life of the Holy Land; over time, their bitter rivalry would help unravel the already fraying social fabric of the settlements.

Relations with the Muslim populations within the Christian states were largely peaceful, although not without periodic friction. The Templars controlled a significant network of castles and military installations throughout the region, especially along the ground transportation routes connecting major cities, which also served as a secure means of communication throughout the kingdom.

After the initial phase of settlement following the conquest, and owing to the persistent divisions among the Muslims, the Christians enjoyed a period of relative peace as exemplified by the contacts between the Templars and Emir Usāma ibn Munqidh. But as early as the mid-twelfth century a process of Islamic revival had begun that would threaten the security of the Christian states of Outremer.

Bernard of Clairvaux

In 1144 the governor of Mosul, Imād ad-Dīn Zangī, attacked the County of Edessa and took possession of the capital after a month-long siege. The defeat reverberated in the West, where many feared for the Christian population in the Holy Land and the crusading ideal itself. The major political powers that could have sent essential reinforcements were experiencing great difficulties of their own. Pope Eugene III (1145–53), successor to Innocent II, was forced to flee Rome after an aristocratic revolt had established a communal government. The rebels threatened to lead an uprising against the papacy inspired by the seething invective of Arnaldo da Brescia against the corruption of the clergy. The appeals for help from overseas reached the pope at his refuge in Viterbo, and he turned to Bernard of Clairvaux for a strategy that would rouse Europe to the new emergency. There were a number of obstacles to overcome. The two most powerful leaders of the West who could have rallied support for the mission, King Louis VII of France and the German king Conrad III (awaiting his coronation as Holy Roman emperor), both faced significant internal opposition to further crusades. As soon as he received the papal letter informing him of the need for an expedition to the East, the French king immediately issued a call to his feudal lords, inviting them to a Christmas meeting in Bourges. Unfortunately, however, he was forced to acknowledge the bitter reality that the nobility of his realm were completely indifferent to the cause. Even his trusted adviser, the authoritative, elderly abbot Suger of Saint-Denis, strongly discouraged the monarch from undertaking the mission. Conrad, the emperor-in-waiting, fared no better. His vassals were engaged in the colonization of Eastern Europe, which they considered a crusade because it involved the conquest of the still-pagan Slavs. Furthermore, some of Conrad's relatives were contesting his right to the title of Holy Roman emperor, and the possibility of his departure for Palestine raised the specter of a revolt.

It wasn't until the end of March 1146 that Louis VII managed to convene a meeting of his barons at Vézelay. The news that Bernard would be speaking there attracted, just as in Clermont half a century before, a crowd so vast that there wasn't enough room in the cathedral, and the abbot was forced to deliver his address from a makeshift stage erected in the open air. Bernard's inspiring advocacy of a second crusade to the Holy Land transformed the crowd. The king had ordered cloth made, from which to cut the crosses that future crusaders would attach to their garments upon taking the solemn vow. But there were so many who answered the call that the abbot and his helpers were still sewing at sunset, when they ran out of cloth. In the fall of that year, while the French were fervidly preparing for their departure, Bernard was invited to speak in the German regions by the archbishops of Cologne and Mainz. In an indefatigable tour of preaching, the abbot went to Freiburg, Basel, Schaffhausen, Constance, and Speyer, where in December 1146 he convinced Conrad III himself to take up the cause.

Templar grand master Everard des Barres organized an effective recruiting program in the West and raised a regiment. In 1147 the crusading army, the largest ever deployed to the Holy Land, made its way to the East. At the point when the German knights were to unite with the French contingent in the lands of the Byzantine Empire, the Templar grand master ably persuaded Emperor Emanuel to welcome the expedition rather than impede it. The emperor feared that the powerful Western force would take over his empire instead of fighting in the crusade. While the army stayed on course, the looting committed by the soldiers deeply angered the emperor. During the passage through the Anatolian high plateau, the Temple was the only contingent to respect the order of march.

Once the crusaders reached Outremer, they immediately engaged the Muslims in battle near Antioch, where the French suffered heavy losses. The Christian front was divided over which strategy to pursue. On June 24, 1148, the king of Jerusalem gathered all the crusader leaders in a great assembly in Acre. The Franks wished to maintain their political alliance with the emir of Damascus, who feared the potential expansion of the small state that Nūr ad-Dīn, a son of the Turkish provincial governor Zangī, had managed to create from the ruins of the County of Edessa. Just twenty-nine years old, Nūr ad-Dīn was a rising political force, and the emir of Damascus hoped to protect his independence through an alliance with the Christians rather than be absorbed by his Muslim neighbor. But the discussions at the assembly in Acre were dominated by special interests and religious notions that had little to do with strategic calculations. The assembly decided to attack Damascus: to the crusaders from the West, Damascus was the site of an event that was fundamental to their faith — the conversion of the Jew Saul to the apostle Paul — and should be in Christian hands. And the wealth of the city proved too tempting for the king of Jerusalem. The attack caused the emir to ally with Nūr ad-Dīn, consolidating the Muslim forces. After just four days, the Christian army was routed and forced to retreat toward

Galilee. In 1148, Conrad III made his way back to Europe through Constantinople, where he struck an agreement with Emperor Emanuel against Roger II of Sicily to divide between them Roger's possessions in Italy. Louis VII remained in Palestine a bit longer, only to leave knowing that he would be returning to the bitterness and political complications of divorce from his beautiful and proud wife, Eleanor of Aquitaine.

During the second crusade, the Templars distinguished themselves with heroism and circumspection, providing models of discipline and skillful diplomatic mediation that further enhanced their reputation. Well trained, loyal to the mission, able to negotiate the complex political tensions of Outremer, the Templars emerged from the failed endeavor with their honor unstained. But the West could not forget that its most powerful Christian army, inspired by a man as extraordinary as Bernard of Clairvaux, had returned from the East in failure.

The Horns of Hattin

The survival of the Christian kingdom in the Holy Land depended on its preventing the Muslim state of Syria to its north from uniting with Fatimid Egypt to its south. While the government of Syria was stable, the reigning dynasty of the Egyptian caliphate had sunk to an alarming level of degradation. The caliph's family had been involved in a sordid history of conspiracy and betrayal that not only weakened the dynasty but allowed one of Nūr ad-Dīn's most enterprising generals, Shīrkūh, to convince the emir of Baghdad to strike against Cairo.

Meanwhile, the king of Jerusalem, Amalric, had his own designs on Egypt, provoking Cairo to seek an alliance with Damascus. This development was exploited by General Shīrkūh's grandson, Saladin. Through a series of successful military campaigns and deft political maneuvers, Saladin managed to take control of Egypt, from where he planned the Islamic reconquest and expulsion of the Christians from the Holy Land.

The enormous wealth of Egypt enabled Saladin to build an empire that stretched from Cyrenaica, in present-day Libya, to the Tigris, in present-day Iraq. He personally presided over the great capitals of Damascus and Aleppo in Syria, which was surrounded by loyal fiefdoms. The caliph of Baghdad supported him, the sultan of Anatolia sought an alliance with him, and the other great Eastern princes had neither the power nor the interest to enter into conflict with him.

The Kingdom of Jerusalem had been profoundly weakened by the terrible misfortune that had struck its young king, Amalric's son Baldwin IV, who was diagnosed with leprosy. Baldwin IV tried arduously to hold on to the reigns of power and defend himself against the intrigues and conspiracies of his own family. In March 1185 he died at the tender age of twenty-four and left his crown to his young nephew, Baldwin V, who died in August 1186 before reaching the age of nine. The political machinations unleashed by the young king's death made the kingdom extremely vulnerable to Muslim conquest.

After sending the regent Raymond of Tripoli to Tiberiade to meet the barons of the realm and devise the procedures for naming a successor to the throne, the Templar seneschal Joscelin occupied Tyre and Beirut and had Sybilla, his niece and the mother of Baldwin V, proclaimed queen. Raymond headed to the castle of Balian d'Ibelin in Nablus, where he convened a meeting of the high court of nobles to certify the legitimacy of his title as regent of the realm. In response, Sybilla ordered the gates of Jerusalem bolted shut and commanded the patriarch of Jerusalem to celebrate her coronation. The royal insignia were kept in a coffer whose keys were in the custody of the patriarch and the grand masters of the Temple and the Hospital of Saint John, but the head of the Hospitallers, indignant at Sybilla's usurpation of the throne, threw his keys out of a window, swearing that neither he nor any of his knights would participate in the ceremony. The patriarch refused to crown Sybilla's husband, Guy de Lusignan, as king because he was hated by the barons and the people alike, so the king's crown was delivered to the new queen for her to bestow on whomever she pleased.

While the Christian kingdom was lacerated by these internal conflicts, Saladin pursued his campaign virtually undisturbed. On July 1, 1187, the sultan crossed the Jordan

River at Sennabra while his troops attacked Tiberiade, which fell after just one hour of combat. Then, perhaps with the assistance of some Christian traitors, he set up camp in the village of Hattin, where there were pastures and an abundant supply of water for his men and their horses. Saladin's position forced the Christian army to march through barren territory, suffering extreme heat and humidity while they defended themselves against continuous attacks on their front and rear guards from bands of Muslim guerillas. By the afternoon of July 3, the Christians had reached the high plateau just above Hattin and stopped for the night near a hill with two peaks, nicknamed the "horns." At dawn, they awoke to find themselves completely surrounded by Saladin's army. At the battle of Hattin, the Christian forces suffered the greatest defeat in the entire history of Outremer. The Templars and Hospitallers fell by the hundreds, and were left by Saladin to the mercy of a ferocious group of Muslim fanatics that had attached themselves to his army.

On September 20, Saladin laid siege to Jerusalem. The city's population had increased due to the influx of refugees seeking shelter there, but the enormous losses suffered in the previous campaigns had so diminished the size of the military contingent that there were now fifty women and children to every man. To satisfy the need for more fighting men, all sons of noble families aged sixteen and older were outfitted as knights; their numbers were later increased by thirty young male commoners. On

October 20, after one month of resistance, the Christians surrendered Jerusalem. With the loss of the city, the seat of the kingdom moved north to Acre.

Less than a century since its conquest, Jerusalem was back in Muslim hands; the Christians would never recapture it. The relic of the True Cross, the most sacred object in Outremer, which a knight from the Temple and one from the Hospital had the honor of escorting in procession, was lost forever.

Saladin showed extraordinary clemency toward the Christian population of Jerusalem, but the sultan deliberately took revenge on the Templars and the Hospitallers for the damage they had inflicted on his army. Arabic sources on the Templars testify to the outstanding technical skill and intense pride of these warriors of God. The historian El-Fadhel transformed the Arabic-Persian word for the Templars, *dawyèh*, into *diwye*, the demon-gods of pagan Mazdeism. Saladin called them "foul people, the worst of the infidels." The massacre of the Templar and Hospitaller knights committed at his orders demonstrated the intense hatred but also the fear that the Muslims felt toward their greatest adversaries.

From the Sepulchre of Christ to the Tomb of Peter

The battle of Hattin inflicted a devastating blow to the Temple: the loss of knights in battle and at the hands of

Saladin had not only decimated the Templars' military force but exacted enormous economic costs as well. War was waged primarily on horseback, and a knight's full coat of armor and standard equipment were extremely expensive. But beyond the economic value of his weaponry was the value of the knight himself, whose technical expertise had been acquired through years of experience and continuous and exhaustive training. The end result, therefore, was a man of rare qualities and qualifications whose skills were obtained only through a considerable financial investment — generally the sole prerogative of the aristocracy.

The continued survival of the order depended on its honor, which inspired generous donations from Christian benefactors to finance the defense of the Holy Land. After Hattin, Templar morale was at an historic low, and the order faced a profound crisis. For the Templars, whose entire raison d'être was the defense of the Holy Land, the fall of Jerusalem and the Holy Sepulchre into Muslim hands represented the failure of their essential purpose.

Furthermore, painful questions weighed on the order. Grand Master Gerard de Ridefort was the only survivor of a group of Templar prisoners who had been captured by Muslims. This was viewed with great suspicion by Western Christendom, the Temple's source of material and spiritual support. Ridefort was a Flemish knight who had arrived in the Holy Land in 1173 and had placed himself at the service of Count Raymond of Tripoli. Capable and ambitious, he soon became invaluable to his lord, who promised him a desirable marriage to the first available suitable heiress. The occasion soon presented itself in the person of Lucia, daughter of the lord of Botrun, who had died without male heirs. But Raymond found it far more profitable to reward another knight named Plivan, who had ensured his claim to the lovely young lady by paying the count her weight in gold. Gerard de Ridefort never forgave his lord for this offense. He joined the order of the Temple, where he soon became known for his martial skills and was quickly promoted to seneschal.

His election as grand master took place between the end of 1184 and the beginning of 1185, after the death of the Spanish grand master, Arnold de Torroja. At that time, the Christian army was in the midst of combating Saladin's advance, while in Jerusalem the leprous king Baldwin IV was languishing near death. Given these circumstances, it is possible that the general chapter of the Temple, normally quite scrupulous in choosing as head of the order a person with a reputation for the utmost transparency, may have given special weight to the military skills of Gerard de Ridefort — a valiant knight, but one who had provided fodder for unfavorable gossip and made influential enemies during his secular life. On military operations, Ridefort was reputedly arrogant and reckless, displaying the typical temperament of the military aristocracy, which Bernard of Clairvaux had tried to discourage and eliminate entirely. In many ways, Ridefort was an anti-Templar; he was antithetical to Bernard's model of the ideal Templar knight. Perhaps the sources of the time amplified his defects to attribute responsibility for the order's defeat to him, but the repeated instances of this negative portrait, which does not afflict the memory of other grand masters, implies that it had some basis in truth.

Intelligent but given to intrigue, Ridefort exploited his relationship with the king of Jerusalem to cast doubt on his former lord, Raymond of Tripoli, subjugating the interests of the Temple to his own desire for revenge. King Henry II of England had donated a substantial sum to the Templars to atone for his guilt in the murder of Thomas Beckett, the archbishop of Canterbury who had insisted on the church's independence from royal interference. The grand master had decided to use part of the money to help the king of Jerusalem recruit four to five thousand foot soldiers for deployment against the advancing Muslims. Ridefort warned the king not to trust Raymond of Tripoli, whom he accused of treason. The king could not contradict him because he feared the powerful Templar to whom he was indebted.

On May 1, 1187, the Christian troops came upon part of Saladin's army at the springs of Cresson, where the Muslims were watering their horses. The grand master of the Hospital and the marshal of the Temple, Jacques de Mailly, prudently advised a retreat since the enemy forces were too numerous to overcome, but Ridefort arrogantly turned his back on the Hospitaller grand master and accused his own marshal of cowardice and vanity, saying, "You love your blond head too much to want to lose it!"

Perhaps because he could no longer control the contempt he felt for his superior, Jacques de Mailly replied, "I will die fighting as a brave man! You, instead, will run away as a traitor!"

The marshal's words proved prophetic, given that only three Templars managed to escape, among them the grand master. When Saladin captured Jersualem a few months later, he ordered the execution of all Templar prisoners — except Ridefort. It was well known that the Muslims tortured Christian prisoners to coerce them to renounce Christ, spit on the cross, and convert to Islam, and it was equally well known that recalcitrant Templars and Hospitallers were beheaded. That the one to escape such an infelicitous fate had been the same man so many had judged an opportunist and a plotter tainted the honor of the Templars; these suspicions dogged the order for some time.

It was thanks to the work of an ingenious man that the Temple was slowly able to recover from its crisis and was rehabilitated in the eyes of Christians. In 1179 the Third Lateran Council discussed usury, which had grown alongside the development of long-distance trade. The council condemned the practice of lending money at interest, and likened moneylenders to thieves deserving of eternal punishment. However, this condemnation did not apply to the Templars, who individually could not possess anything beyond the pitiful sum of four dinars and who dedicated all of their revenues to the defense of the Holy Land.

Pope Innocent III made abundant use of the Temple as a bank in service to the crusades because of the brothers' considerable financial skills and their irreproachable reputation for honesty. In doing so, the pope performed a work of invaluable propaganda for the order, and he was soon imitated by sovereigns and powerful families throughout Europe. The pontiff also attempted to make induction into the order less exclusive. The perilous situation in the Holy Land necessitated massive recruitment in the West, but the requirements for the Templar knight were so exacting and the order's discipline so rigid that only a select minority of nobles had the characteristics suited for membership.

Innocent III, working closely with the ranking clergy of Outremer, who had direct knowledge of local conditions, began by opening the ranks of the Templars to men who previously would not have been admitted. He issued various acts to relax the order's harsh disciplinary code without betraying its ideals. It was during his pontificate that the Templar rule, originally written in Latin, was translated into French. The new version included one important modification: excommunicated knights, who previously could not so much as be approached by the brothers of the Temple, were now welcomed into the order so long as they had confessed their sins and received absolution. This may have been part of the effort to adapt to the changing times, as the rigid spirituality of Bernard of Clairvaux gradually gave way to an attitude more open to compassion and forgiveness. Or perhaps it was the product of a pragmatic calculation no different from that which had led Pope Urban II to call violent knights to the first crusade more than one hundred years earlier. These marginal knights were "recuperated" for the faith and proved useful to society. In light of such considerations, it seems logical to blame the gradual decline of the Temple over the course of the thirteenth century to this softening of its disciplinary code, but this conclusion is mistaken. The change in the Templar ethic during the last decades of the life of the order derived from more recent and more serious problems that the order's leadership either would not or could not contain.

In fact, the pope's concessions saved the Temple from the danger of rapid extinction by restoring its economic vigor and by boosting its recruitment efforts. Innocent III, more than his predecessors, succeeded in establishing a close bond between the Holy See and the order, by turning it, together with the Order of the Knights Hospitaller, into a pontifical militia with absolute loyalty to the papacy. The defense of the faith would include support for orthodoxy under the tutelage of the papacy — the very symbol of Christianity now that the Holy City had fallen back under Muslim control, but an institution also threatened by the spread of heresy and attacks from its political enemies. From then on, the Templars defined the Roman pontiff as "our Apostolic Father, lord and master of the Temple after our Lord Jesus Christ." Having lost Jerusalem and awaiting the recovery of the Holy Sepulchre, the Temple undertook its own reconstruction.

The Tragedy of the Fourth Crusade

The dramatic defeat at Hattin created a sense of religious and political impotence to which the sovereign dynasties and great feudal lords of Europe could not resign themselves. In 1189 the third crusade was launched to recapture the Holy Land from Saladin. It was led by the most powerful monarchs of Europe — King Richard the Lionhearted of England, King Philip Augustus II of France, and Holy Roman Emperor Frederick Barbarossa. The elderly Barbarossa died before reaching the Holy Land. The crusaders pushed on and engaged Saladin's army, but after numerous battles over a three-year period, the Christians failed to reclaim Jerusalem. On September 2, 1192, Richard the Lionhearted signed a treaty with Saladin that left Jerusalem in Muslim hands but allowed Christian pilgrims to visit the Holy City freely and safely. The treaty effectively ended the third crusade.

In 1199 a zealous preacher named Fulk of Neuilly presented himself at the castle of Ecry sur-Aisne, where several great French feudal lords were entertaining themselves at a jousting tournament hosted by Count Theobald of Champagne. Fulk's passionate sermons moved their noble lordships, rousing once again the nostalgic vision of conquering the opulent and mysterious East and recapturing the Holy Sepulchre for Christendom. In February 1200 the movement won the hearts of the counts of Flanders, and several delegations traveled to Italy to craft an agreement with Venice, which would furnish the ships needed to transport the crusaders to the East. Pope Innocent III, who had been working actively toward retaking Jerusalem, blessed the initiative and fostered it by granting spiritual favors and tax exemptions.

By August 1202 the crusaders were finally gathered in Venice, but there were many fewer than had been planned, and the money they had raised, 50,000 marks, was far less than the amount previously agreed upon to pay for the voyage. The Venetian shipyards had been working for many months to build the necessary ships at an enormous expenditure of material and specialized labor, for which the leaders of the crusade were unable to pay. They blamed a handful of feudal lords who had deserted the enterprise and taken their financial contributions with them. The lofty goal of recovering the Holy Sepulchre — for which the flower of French nobility had mobilized and was now left humiliated, amassed on the shore, awaiting some sudden event that might save them from the shame of immediately returning home — remained unrealized. These lords had personally assumed and imposed on their vassals huge expenses to organize the expedition with the prospect of conquering new lands in the East, only to be prevented and frustrated.

At the time, the Byzantine imperial dynasty was in a greatly weakened condition following the considerable stability it had achieved for most of the twelfth century under the reign of the Comnenus emperors. In 1195, Emperor Isaac II Angelus was dethroned by his brother, who was then forced to defend himself from plots by other members of the family. In 1201 young Alexis, son of the dethroned emperor, traveled to the West and implored the leaders of the crusade to stop in Constantinople, overthrow the usurper, and restore his father to the throne. Prior to these talks, Alexis had visited the pope, promising to reunite the Greek and Latin churches, separated since the great schism in 1054, in exchange for his assistance. But the pope knew the long history of the many intrigues and conflicts that troubled the Byzantine imperial court and felt it wise not to become involved in its internal dynastic contest. Furthermore, Innocent III's fundamental interest was the reconquest of Jerusalem.

The unresolved situation of the crusaders on the Venetian shore presented an opportunity for various interests to come together. Venice, which had its sights set on territorial expansion in the Adriatic Sea, accepted the proposal that the crusaders pay for their voyage after achieving their first victories, on condition that on the way to Jerusalem they stop at Zara to conquer that city and restore it to Venetian rule. The economic interests of the crusaders quickly superceded the religious quest to retake the Holy City, turning the fourth crusade into an operation of conquest and pure profit accomplished at the expense of Constantinople, the opulent capital of the Byzantine Empire. The Latin Christians laid siege to the city, and after sacking it, installed a new imperial dynasty of French blood that would rule Byzantium for more than fifty years (1204–61).

Pope Innocent III excommunicated the crusaders and the rulers of Venice after the slaughter in Zara, an attack on fellow Christians that had nothing to do with the reconquest of the Holy Land. He later decided to pardon the French knights inasmuch as they had been obliged to commit their violent acts by the blackmail pact imposed on them by the Venetians, whom he left without absolution, judging them to be the true culprits. After the sack and occupation of Constantinople, Innocent III recognized the authority of the new Latin emperor in order to end the schism. The pope ordered the new emperor to ensure that the Latin rite took root throughout the territories of the Byzantine Empire. To support this objective, he also installed in the area the three orders in which he had the most trust: the Templars, the Hospitallers, and the Cistercians. The two military orders took possession of various fiefdoms in the Byzantine territories, a concession looked upon with disfavor by the emperor and his vassals. In their view, the Templars and the Hospitallers, not having participated in the taking of Constantinople, had no rights over the conquered lands.

While on a purely political level the fourth crusade had amply furthered the interests of most of its participants, on every other level it was a huge disaster. It was a failure for Innocent III, who begrudgingly accepted the unexpected results of the expedition not because he was consoled by the unification of the church but because he continued to delude himself up to the very end that the Western conquest of Byzantium was the harbinger of the reconquest of Jerusalem. The fourth crusade undermined the very ideals that had inspired it in the first place, effectively demonstrating that base self-interest could corrupt even the best of intentions.

The Excommunicated Emperor and the Holy King

In 1215, the year before his death, Innocent III called for the fifth crusade, convincing his pupil Frederick II, son of Emperor Henry VI and grandson of Barbarossa, to take up the cross at Aquisgrana. The new pope, Honorius III, fulfilled the commitment of his predecessor and raised a massive army, which was joined by the king of Hungary. But young Frederick II was so occupied with his political enemies in Germany and Italy that the expedition set off without him. Some ten years after taking the vow, the Holy Roman emperor committed himself anew, but he disappointed the pope once again by merely sending a fleet to Acre to bring back his bride, Yolande of Brienne. In 1227 the solicitations of the new pope, Gregory IX, finally succeeded in getting the emperor to undertake the voyage, but after boarding at Otranto, Frederick II immediately disembarked because an epidemic had broken out on the ship. This latest withdrawal, some twelve years after the original vow, infuriated Gregory IX, who interpreted it as a complete lack of interest in the crusade. The pope retaliated by punishing the emperor with excommunication. In June 1228, when Frederick finally left at the head of the sixth crusade, it was without papal approval. He was the excommunicated leader of an expedition that was launched to liberate the Holy Sepulchre — the ultimate paradox.

In the Holy Land, Frederick managed what no other Christian leader had done in the previous forty years. He negotiated a treaty with al-Kamil — the nephew of Saladin and sultan of Egypt, with whom the emperor, a great admirer of Islamic culture, had established a good relationship — for Christian control over Jerusalem, Bethlehem, and Nazareth for ten years. However, the Temple Mount, al-Aqsa Mosque, and the Dome of the Rock remained in Muslim hands. The sultan also extracted a promise that no Western prince would plan an attack along the Nile. In March 1229, Frederick II made his triumphal entrance into the Church of the Holy Sepulchre and took the crown of King of Jerusalem, a title he claimed on behalf of his infant son, the rightful king. The religious authorities in the Holy Land, including the patriarch of Jerusalem, refused to recognize his coronation. Neither did the Templars, who would not acknowledge the legitimacy of any sovereign excommunicated by the pope. Frederick II disdained the Templars, considering them a band of fanatics. Despite his many critics, however, Frederick II had successfully restored Jerusalem to Christian hands, if only temporarily.

In 1239, at the end of the ten-year truce, a new contingent of crusaders left Europe with the intention of retaking Jerusalem by force. The Arab potentate of Damascus controlled the city, but the following year the king of Navarre, one of the leaders of the new expedition, realized that Frederick II's strategy had its advantages. He began working toward obtaining protection over Jerusalem through diplomatic means. His efforts appeared to have a good chance of success when suddenly, in 1244, a column of Turks in service to Egypt inflicted a devastating defeat on the Christians at La Forbie, from which they would never fully recover. Any hope of reclaiming the Holy City continued to drift further and further away.

In 1245 a great ecumenical council met in Lyon, where Pope Innocent IV reiterated the absolute necessity of making a new commitment to the Christians in Outremer. His call was answered by the French king Louis IX, who was of an ascetic cast of mind, endowed with profound spirituality, and inclined to mysticism. While the rest of Europe remained unresponsive to the pope's pleas to address the emergency in the Holy Land, convinced that it was almost impossible to break up the compact Muslim alliance between Syria-Palestine and Egypt, the young king set off on the seventh crusade in 1248. After a stop in Cyprus to finalize his strategy, Louis IX attacked Egypt at Damietta, successfully occupying the city. At that point, the most prudent move would have been to strike the powerful Egyptian city of Alexandria, which would have ensured the crusaders possession of an important stronghold from which to launch a campaign for the conquest of the hinterland. But the king, badly advised and perhaps a man of a rather unpragmatic nature, let himself be convinced to move against Cairo. In December he had gone as far as al-Mansūra, but there the Christian troops were forced into a war of attrition among the canals of the Nile, which ended in a crushing defeat that saw the king and his brothers taken prisoner by the Muslims. Released in 1254 after paying a large ransom, Louis IX resigned himself to returning home. By then the West had lost interest in the enterprise, and his mother, Blanche of Castile, acting as regent for her absent son, had sparked a rebellion in his kingdom.

Over the course of the 1260s, the rise of another charismatic Muslim military leader, the sultan Baibars I, heralded the declining fortunes of what remained of the Christian kingdom in the Holy Land. Rukn ad-Din Baibars was a

Kipchak Turk of enormous physical stature, whose dark skin was in stark contrast to his blue eyes. He had been brought to Syria as a young slave and sold to the emir of Hama. The emir thought he was too coarse for the court, but noting his physical strength and intelligence, the emir offered Baibars to the sultan as a member of the Mameluke guard. Baibars shone in his new role, and after his victory over the Christians in 1244 at La Forbie, he became legendary. After seizing power first in Egypt and then in Damascus between 1265 and 1272, he occupied the remaining Christian strongholds, reducing Outremer to a minuscule area around Acre. Caesarea, Haifa, and Arsuf all fell quickly, followed by the wealthy city of Jaffa and the Templar castle of Beaufort. In the spring of 1266, the principality of Antioch also succumbed; the first of the Christian states founded in the Holy Land, it had managed to repulse Muslim attacks for 171 years. Inevitably, Baibars's next move would be to launch an attack against the Christian outpost of Acre.

Inspired to action by the tragic news from the East, King James I of Aragon and King Louis IX of France set off on the eighth crusade. James I left Barcelona with a powerful fleet, but it was badly damaged in a storm, and he was forced to return. His two illegitimate sons completed the voyage with what remained of the fleet and met up with the rest of the Christian contingent. Louis IX left from Aigues Mortes in July 1270, together with his brother Charles I of Anjou, king of Sicily. Charles, however, was more interested in diverting the expedition toward Constantinople in order to recover the Byzantine throne that Emperor Michael VIII Paleologus had taken in 1261.

Louis IX disembarked at Carthage and headed for Tunisia, seeking an alliance with the sultan of Tunis. The king was misled by the mistaken belief that the sultan's conversion to Christianity would guarantee his strong support for the Christians against Egypt. But in 1270 illness broke out among the troops and struck the king, who died on August 25. Charles of Anjou took command and exploited what little results had been achieved to force the sultan of Tunis to pay him tribute as king of Sicily. Charles returned to Europe, followed by the rest of the Christian contingent, which dispersed as soon as it reached the coast of Sicily.

Courtier Gossip

The Order of the Knights Templar had always had enemies even more insidious than the Muslim marauders whom it had been created to fight. The special concessions given to the order by Pope Innocent II in *Every Perfect Gift*, which were extended by successive pontiffs, had clothed the Temple with political and legal autonomy. High-ranking clerics in the areas where the order's most important houses were located were jealous of the warrior-monks' complete independence from the church hierarchy. Although the Templars were exempt from taxation, the Western branch of the order periodically paid the church one-tenth of its income as a tithe, which in the era of the crusades was funneled by the pope back into the military efforts in the East. A donation to the Temple amounted to a donation to the crusades.

In the twelfth century, the Western economy was predominantly agricultural, with an emerging commercial sector. The Templar houses ran a network of high-yield farms, each producing a different range of products, depending on the qualities of the local soil and climate. Arms and horses were needed for the defense of the Holy Land, but consumer goods, apart from certain foods, could not tolerate the long voyage to the East. The Templars were forced to convert these goods into money, which their fame as warriors protected against the threat of piracy on the high seas. Once they reached Outremer, the transported sums were used to buy food, cattle, and other provisions. It was vital that these operations not be conducted at a loss, that they take into account the possibility of damage from shipwrecks and other disasters, and that they produce a profit sufficient to cover the risks. The products of Templar farms sold in European markets were usually cheaper because the order enjoyed favorable tax exemptions other producers did not; the prices of Templar goods were very competitive.

The large Templar family comprised not only the professed brother-knights but a multitude of people who had requested and obtained affiliation with the order, supported it with their donations, and regularly attended Templar churches, where they received the sacraments and, when possible, even burial. There developed a vocation in extremis, instituted for those whose responsibilities prevented them from joining the order but who desired to die as a Templar. These men could profess their vows on their deathbeds, becoming brothers of the Temple if only for a short time, and receiving upon their death all the honors and prayers customarily reserved for their brethren. Donations from Templars in extremis and those affiliated with the order were bound to invite envy among members of other orders and in the secular church. Even attendance by the faithful at Templar churches brought the order the benefit of their weekly offerings, which otherwise would have gone to cathedrals, parishes, and monasteries.

These substantial privileges had already provoked resentment in the mid-twelfth century, when the Templars were at the peak of their power. But at that time Western society supported the order with unswerving passion, and the glory of its name made its detractors look like a tiny minority driven by petty rancor.

In the second half of the twelfth century, the first authoritative voice of dissent raised amid the chorus of praise for the Templars belonged to Archbishop William of Tyre. Born in the Holy Land around 1130, he traveled to Italy — learning Latin, Greek, and Arabic along the way — and took his sacred vows before becoming ambassador to the court of Constantinople and then chancellor of the Kingdom of Jerusalem. Around 1173, on orders from King Amalric, he composed an important work entitled *The History of Outremer*; barely two years later he was appointed archbishop of Tyre. Although he was a competent historian who drew on archival documents to write a factual account, William was a harsh critic of the Templars. As a ranking cleric in the Holy Land, he reproached them for their complete independence from the church hierarchy of Outremer. An extremely important, though not always objective source for reconstructing the history of the order from its inception, William's *History* presents a heroic image of the first Templars — poor, humble, and penitent — only to conclude that their successors' excessive accumulation of wealth and privileges had made them proud and lax.

Walter Map, a cleric in the entourage of the king of England, was another critic of the Templars, who occupied a significant place in the polemics against the military orders. Born in 1140, Map was largely ignorant of affairs in the East, but his ample production of poetry and satire included a number of attacks on the vices of the military orders. He was especially censorious of the Templars' arrogance and wealth, which he considered contrary to the original spirit of the order. Map was the author of a work entitled *De nugis curialum*, or *Courtiers' Trifles*. Satirical and decidedly caustic in tone, this collection of portraits, legends, and tales spared no one, but its irony was aimed most fiercely at the clergy, from country priests to the pope. Map's critique left its mark on the culture of the time because his acerbic observations were penetrating and not without merit.

During the early thirteenth century, as the hope of retaking Jerusalem became increasingly more remote, polemical attacks against the military orders charged with the defense of the Holy Land grew more intense. More important, they were no longer confined to the gossip and idle chatter of courtiers. The harshest ideological attack directed at the Temple at the time was by a monk from the abbey of Saint Albans, Matthew Paris. An authoritative figure known not only as a writer but also as a painter and goldsmith, he enjoyed the favor of King Henry III of England, who often sought his counsel on important political and ecclesiastical matters. He also had the esteem of Pope Innocent IV, who in 1248 sent him on a mission to Norway to reform the abbey of Saint Benet Holm. Paris distinguished himself for the courage and vivacity with which he treated the events of his time, thanks to his vast experience in the political sphere. Matthew Paris's *Chronica maior*, considered by many scholars as the best English account of the period, is a stinging critique of society and the clergy. It includes bitter commentary on the king and his favorite courtiers, but his criticisms of the Templars are among the harshest. The golden age of the order, the glorious epoch in which all of Christian society identified the Templars as heroes of the faith and guardians of the most sacred sites and relics of Christendom, was nearing its end.

From Lyon to Cyprus

Baibars's continuous victories drew pointed reprobation against the Temple, some originating from within the order itself, which was demoralized by its repeated military defeats. After one such defeat, and perhaps driven in part by resentment toward the leadership of the order, Templar poet Ricaut Bonomel composed the song "I're dolors" ("Anger and Grief"). Its harsh tone allows us to understand the levels of anger and frustration that afflicted the warrior-brothers:

> Anger and grief have so filled my heart
> that I am on the verge of killing myself;
> or of laying down the cross I had taken up
> in honor of Him Who was put on the Cross;
> For neither cross nor faith brings me aid or protection
> against the treacherous Turks, God damn them!
> On the contrary it seems, from what one can see,
> that God wishes to assist them to our detriment. . . .
> So then he who leads the battle against the Turks is a
>   total fool

since Jesus Christ does not at all oppose them.
Indeed they have won and continue to win, giving me
    great pain,
Franks and Tartars, Armenians and Persians.
And here every day they taste victory over us
because God, Who used to keep vigil, has gone to sleep.
And Mohammed brings to bear all of his forces
goading Baibars into action
It does not seem for now that he will ever give up
    the fight,
Rather he has sworn and openly declared
that if he has his way not even one man
who believes in Jesus Christ will be left in this land:
that on the contrary he will turn
the church of Saint Mary into a mosque.
And since Her Son, Who should be grieved
Wants and approves all of this, it must please us as well.

After Baibars had reduced Outremer to a remnant of the former realm, the military orders became a troubling issue of foreign policy debated in all the courts of Europe. Western society — which had tolerated the orders' privileges and, at times, their overbearing arrogance, in deference to their role as defenders of the Holy Land — was no longer willing to abide their failures. There were discussions on how best to restore the operational capabilities of the Templars and Hospitallers to their former levels. Some argued that merging the two into one order would reduce expenses, improve efficiency, and eliminate an annoying problem for which both were responsible: the continuous rivalry that, whether real or exaggerated by their denigrators, had helped complicate the already difficult circumstances of the Latin presence in the East.

In the Kingdom of Jerusalem the power and prestige enjoyed by the two orders were of equal measure, the one being charged with forming the advance guard and the other the rear guard of the Christian army. The high honor of escorting in processions the most sacred relic of the kingdom, a fragment of the wood of the True Cross, belonged to Templar and Hospitaller alike. The leadership of both orders were consulted on the most important questions affecting the kingdom, but too often they took opposing positions on pressing political issues.

Neither the Templars nor the Hospitallers had refrained from involvement in the tensions, plots, and machinations that had troubled the Christian states of Outremer. The dynastic wars had been waged with the active participation of both orders, which had vested interests in ensuring the victory of a sovereign favorable to them. Far from remaining a local concern in the East, the echo of these intrigues had reached the pope and the other rulers of Europe, damaging the reputation of both orders.

The most widely held opinion was that the Templars and Hospitallers owed their moral decay to their forced absence from combat. It was urgent, therefore, that they be restored to the vigor and glory that had distinguished them in the past. In 1274, Pope Gregory X (Theobald Visconti, 1272–77) called a council at Lyon to resolve the crisis in Outremer and to discuss the reunification of the Greek and Latin churches. Before he became pope, Theobald had participated in the eighth crusade led by Louis IX. On seeing it end with the death of the king, he accompanied to Palestine Prince Edward of England, who led the ninth crusade. In late spring of 1271, Theobald landed in Acre only to depart three months later, when he learned of his election to the papacy.

The question of the unification of the Temple and the Hospital was debated at Lyon. The grand masters of the two military orders were consulted, and both expressed their absolute opposition to the merger. The grand master of the Temple, Thomas Bérard, drafted an effective response in which — while emphasizing that the Temple was subject to the pope and that his men would obey the pope's will — he denounced the merger as an expedient proposal made by the European crowns to ensure themselves control over the orders in their respective realms. The grand masters' position was supported by King James I of Aragon. Forced to defend his kingdom against his bellicose Muslim neighbors, who controlled the southern part of the Iberian peninsula, the king had always promoted the growth of the two military orders. However, James I believed that if the merger were approved, the new unified order would be so economically and militarily powerful as to constitute a serious political threat to the crown. The opposition of the king and the two grand masters, followed closely by the death of the crusader pope, forced the proposal to be tabled.

In 1291, the fall of Acre, the last Christian stronghold in the Holy Land, spelled the demise of Outremer. The Templars and Hospitallers retreated to Cyprus, an island northwest of Acre; its position made it an excellent vantage point from which to observe the situation in Syria-Palestine and plan new military interventions.

The grand master of the Temple, Guillaume de Beaujeu, a member of one of the most eminent French noble families and a magnificent example of chivalric values and Christian virtues, had died in the effort to save Acre. He was buried by his comrades in the church of the order just before the Templars, the last to do so, abandoned the city in flames. But neither the glorious reputation of Beaujeu, famous for his heroism and for his many public and private donations, nor the honorable conduct of the Templars could erase the bitter truth: the Holy Land was lost, and the era of the crusades was over.

In the West, this stunning and final defeat brought the proposal to merge the two military orders back to the fore. The advisers of Charles II of Anjou drew up a plan that required the head of the unified order to be the son of a Christian royal family invested with a claim to the lost throne of Jerusalem. The great Catalonian philosopher Ramon Lull proposed calling the new entity the Order of the Holy Spirit and recommended, with respect to the vow of chastity observed by the brothers of the Temple and the Hospital, that the future leader be a celibate or widowed king. In 1292, at the Council of Arles, Pope Nicholas IV issued a decree that the Order of the Knights Templar and the Order of the Knights Hospitaller be united, but the obstacles to the merger and the death of the pontiff prevented its implementation.

V

Between a Rock and a Hard Place: The Papacy, Philip the Fair, and Jacques de Molay

The Manifesto of Lunghezza

The death of Pope Nicholas IV on April 2, 1292, only a year after the fall of Acre, had thwarted efforts to resolve the crisis in the East and reconcile the Greek and Roman churches. The pontiff had close ties to the aristocratic Colonna family, who had unscrupulously exploited papal favor to pursue its own interests, causing widespread scandal. Gathered to elect a new pope, the cardinals agreed on the need to choose a profoundly spiritual personality, even at the cost of less refined political and administrative skills, in order to curb the ills that had afflicted the papacy most intensely — particularly nepotism and simony.

At the beginning of the thirteenth century, the Franciscan friar Joachim of Fiore prophesied the advent of a new era characterized by the domination of the spirit, which would be inaugurated by the election of an "angelic pope," a perfectly holy man who would lead the church out of the crisis. Compelled by Joachim's prophesy and by a desire for reform, the College of Cardinals selected as the new pope the Franciscan hermit Peter of Morrone, who lived in perpetual retreat and was considered by many well on his way to sainthood. The newly elected pope, who took the name of Celestine V, accepted the office only under heavy pressure from the cardinals and from his favorite spiritual son, the king of Naples, Charles II of Anjou. But the hermit, who was forced from his cave to supervise the complex political and administrative mechanisms of the Curia, soon found himself out of his depth. The church was an enormous multinational organization that required superior management expertise and an ample capacity for diplomacy. Peter of Morrone was profoundly ill at ease taking political initiatives, which required making choices and assuming responsibilities that disturbed his ascetic frame of mind.

Feeling himself utterly inadequate, Celestine V trusted in the capacity of his closest advisers, but his great inexperience led him to promote to high office men of rather dubious reputation. Shortly after his election, even King Charles II of Anjou, who had done so much to support his candidacy, had to admit that the good hermit's political and diplomatic ineptitude had become a burden to the church.

Church leaders were forced to address the question: Did canon law allow papal abdication? The best jurists of the age — Vatican insiders Cardinal Benedict Caetani and Cardinal Jean Lemoine, as well as Peter John Olivi of the Spirituals, a radical congregation of Franciscans who espoused a return to the strict rule of Saint Francis — were consulted. Despite their contrasting visions of the world and the church, these three eminent jurists concurred that papal renunciation of the pontifical throne was possible because there was a difference between *apostolic charisma* — the gift of grace from the Holy Spirit to the successors of Christ's apostles, which would remain in the man — and the *apostolic function* — the continuation of the work of the apostles — which he would be abdicating.

Desperate to restore the office of the papacy to its normal activities after it had been all but paralyzed during the five months of Celestine V's pontificate, the cardinals ratified the decree of abdication and proceeded to elect as his successor the most able among their ranks. Benedict Caetani took the name of Boniface VIII (1294–1303). The new pope was quite expert in the things of the world, but he was greatly maligned by the illustrious poets Jacopone da Todi and Dante Alighieri, who were his political enemies.

Like Peter John Olivi, Jacopone was a member of the Spirituals. Shortly after taking office, Pope Boniface VIII revoked the privilege granted to the Spirituals by Celestine V, which allowed them to live apart from the rest of their Franciscan brethren. Boniface considered their desire for autonomy an expression of moral condemnation of their own order. The pope provoked Dante's hatred when he supported the Blacks, a Florentine political faction, in a war against their rivals, the Whites. The victory of the Blacks caused Dante, a member of the White faction, to be exiled from his beloved Florence. The poet exacted revenge by condemning Boniface to hell in *The Divine Comedy*.

Boniface VIII belonged to one of the most powerful families of the Roman aristocracy. He was an illustrious jurist and had served for many years in the diplomatic corps of the Holy See, earning admiration for his skills as a mediator. His election was swift; agreement was reached almost immediately by the College of Cardinals, including Cardinals Peter and James Colonna, whose family was in a bitter rivalry with the Caetanis. For the first few years of his reign, the Colonnas actively cooperated with the new pope in running the Curia. But then, in 1297 a serious incident shattered the peace.

When Boniface VIII was elected, the coffers of the papacy were empty, so he ordered a sizable withdrawal of funds from the family headquarters in Anagni and asked that the money be brought to Rome. Along the way, a band led by a member of the Colonna family assaulted the convoy, and absconded with the gold as well as the mules. Boniface VIII immediately summoned the Colonna cardinals to hold them responsible for the theft, but instead of presenting themselves to the pope they fled to Lunghezza, where they wrote and distributed an article of denunciation. This document, known as the "Manifesto of Lunghezza," claimed that several illicit acts were committed during the election of Boniface VIII, which threatened to undermine his legitimacy as pope.

The Armed Guard of the Roman Church

In 1294 the French king Philip IV, also known as Philip the Fair, attacked the fiefdom of Gascony, a large and rich territory in southwestern France, in order to annex it to his realm. The move unleashed a bitterly fought war with King Edward I of England, the titleholder of the fiefdom. Philip's move was a sharp break from the policy of his grandfather, King Louis IX. Louis's solution, called the "feudal compromise," obliged the king of England to take an oath of loyalty; as the lord of Gascony, he was a vassal of the king of France. By the end of the thirteenth century, however, profound changes in society and in the political strategy of the French court made the pact devised by Louis IX seem outdated. Times were moving rapidly toward the secularization of power and the affirmation of nationstates, and before long many of the fundamental elements of the old medieval political order would be swept aside.

The high cost of the war over Gascony drove Philip the Fair and Edward to take a drastic measure: they taxed the clergy in their respective realms, in violation of privileges that granted religious orders exemption from taxation. The protests of the clergy reached Pope Boniface VIII, who immediately admonished the two monarchs that church property could not serve to satisfy the interests of secular power and threatened them with excommunication.

The French objected strongly to the papal pronouncement, viewing it as an attempt to block a legitimate and necessary act in the interests of the realm. There followed a fierce dispute over the rights of the crown versus the rights of the papacy, which ventured far beyond the issue of taxation. While Boniface VIII defended the traditional theocratic concept that gave the pope, as the vicar of Christ on earth, the right and duty to correct royal excesses, Philip the Fair responded with a new ideology that held that a prince was sovereign in his realm, an authority completely independent of any other power: *superiorem non recognoscens* (recognizes no superior).

After the initial heated exchanges, the debate gradually moved toward a search for concrete solutions to the problem at hand. A delegation of French clergy went to Rome to inform the pope about the critical financial state of the realm, asking him to respond positively to the king's needs. Boniface VIII softened his position, affirming that a secular king could not impinge on the rights of the church but allowing him to impose taxes on the clergy of the realm when necessary to save the country in an emergency. To seal the peace agreement to the satisfaction of both parties, the pope approved the canonization of Louis IX, which his grandson Philip IV so ardently desired.

With the French problem resolved, the pope turned to matters of internal dissent. By 1298, Boniface VIII found himself in financial difficulties caused by his conflict with the Colonnas. He turned to the Temple and the Hospital for assistance, arguing that such financial support was among their duties. The military orders had taken a vow to defend the faith, and now the faith required protection from the two schismatic cardinals who were attacking the church by questioning the legitimacy of its leader.

The Temple obeyed immediately and without discussion, loyal to the precept of its rule that the pope was the master of the order after Christ himself. The Hospital sent a lesser sum; the pope expressed no resentment, save to comment that the amount requested had been provided primarily by the Templars.

With the loss of the Holy Land, the Templars were no longer as useful as they once were. But by responding generously to the pope's request, they demonstrated that they would remain an important presence in Christian society, a bulwark of support for the papacy.

War Games: The Owl and the Warlock

In 1301 the already strained relationship between Boniface VIII and Philip the Fair took a dramatic turn for the worse. Bernard Saisset, bishop of the French diocese of Pamiers, spoke out against a series of abuses committed by the king at the expense of the French clergy. In his judgment, the king was a magnificent puppet in the hands of his ministers. "Our sovereign greatly resembles the royal owl, the most beautiful of all birds, but it is worth nothing. The only thing he knows how to do is stare at people, without talking."

Taciturn, withdrawn, and mourning the death of his wife, Philip IV was so rigidly religious that he bordered on fanaticism. The king effectively allowed his appointed ministers to act in his stead, and he may have given the impression of great moral severity coupled with political ineptitude.

The bishop's pronouncements were not unfounded. Historians seem to agree that Philip the Fair had gradually abandoned his real power, leaving the government of the country to the lawyers on his royal council. However, the French cleric's outspokenness coincided with dangerous disputes within the royal court itself. Bernard Saisset was accused of high treason and condemned to death by order of the king. But Philip had not consulted the pope, who, according to the law, was the only authority with the right to judge a cleric. The inevitable papal reaction set off a heated conflict with the French crown.

Boniface VIII was a troublesome pope for two reasons. He had several undeniable human weaknesses that stood in stark contrast to the "angelic" qualities of his predecessor, Celestine V: ambition, a relish for power and pomp, a grandiose vision of his role as head of the church that led him to enhance certain theatrical aspects of the office. One example was the stupefying metamorphosis of the papal tiara, which Boniface VIII transformed from a simple, if elegant, crown into an ostentatious display of gold and gems, topped with an oversized ruby of incalculable value. But it was neither the pope's taste for luxury nor his other human faults that worried the Council of France. The second reason was far more serious.

Like the Colonnas, Philip IV's men understood that in order for the crown to function without papal interference, they would have to remove Boniface. His election, coming on the heels of Celestine V's abdication, or the "great refusal," took place in circumstances absolutely unprecedented in the history of the church. This gave Boniface's enemies the grounds to argue that his pontificate was not legitimate.

The heart of the problem was that Boniface VIII, faithful to the theocratic tradition, conceived of the church as the dominant institution in both the spiritual and temporal realms, and he strenuously defended its sovereign prerogatives. The royal council was in the process of elaborating an ideology in which France claimed the political leadership of Christian society. Philip's lawyers asserted that the French monarch was descended from the blessed dynasty of Clovis, who according to tradition had been anointed with a miraculous oil that the Holy Spirit, in the guise of a dove, had brought down from heaven. Therefore, the kings of France derived their sovereignty directly from the will of God and their dignity was spiritually superior to that of all other rulers. Thus, according to these

French ideologues, it was right and just that their king should have political primacy over all of Christendom, since he, the most Christian king, would be best able to lead it to salvation by curing it of all its ills. Here was the classic battle between church and state.

The political argument advanced by the pope's French adversaries was strengthened by his two bitter enemies, the Colonna cardinals, who claimed that he had appropriated the apostolic office through deception and that his election was invalid. The "Colonna thesis" became extremely useful to the Council of France; it helped win the support of the French clergy for the council's proposal to depose Boniface VIII and elect another, more compliant, pope. Philip the Fair's jurists portrayed the king as the savior of Christian civilization, a shepherd of Christ's flock in competition with the usurper of Saint Peter's throne. Since this legal argument was not enough to demonstrate that Boniface's pontificate was an unfortunate error of the church that should be erased as soon as possible, the crown's lawyers misrepresented some of the pope's ideas, which he had expressed in private or in an unofficial capacity. They distorted the true meaning of the dogma of papal infallibility, sanctioned by Boniface VIII in his bull *Unam sanctam* (*The One Holy*), which they used as the basis to spread the rumor that the pope was bound to a strange demon whom he evoked and interrogated and from whom he received superior knowledge and the capacity never to err.

From the simple beneficiary of a canonically debatable election, Benedict Caetani was gradually transformed into a warlock-pope.

Boniface VIII responded by preparing a bull of excommunication against the king of France entitled *Super Petri solio*. The pope intended to publish the bull on September 8, 1303, but an expedition of French soldiers led by Guillaume de Nogaret, the best known of the jurists on the council, joined a band of Colonna supporters near the city of Anagni, where Boniface was staying. On the night of September 7, they assaulted the pope and attempted to take him prisoner and transport him to Paris, where he would be deposed and declared a heretic. A spontaneous uprising by the people of Anagni, who were enraged by the looting of the Colonnas' soldiers, freed the pope, who was taken back to Rome. Despite the successful rescue operation, Boniface VIII never recovered from that terrible night. He died shortly thereafter. Although the papal bull excommunicating Philip the Fair and stripping him of all his powers was never published, it became a sword of Damocles hanging over the king in the years to come.

The Two-Headed Monster

With the irrevocable loss of the Holy Land, the Temple successfully completed its transformation into a financial powerhouse. The order served as a bank to the pope and other European rulers; its general headquarters in Paris became the treasury of the French crown. The growth of its financial operations resulted in substantial changes in the Temple's internal balance of power.

In the early days of the order, true Templars were *milites*, professionals of war on horseback drawn from the ranks of the chivalric elite; those who provided other services were relegated to the lower level of sergeant. In order to prosper in the tasks that the times had forced upon them, that is, the custody and investment of funds raised to finance the crusades, the Temple needed accountants, administrators, and notaries. These activities required a technical and practical education typical of bourgeois families engaged in commerce, an activity disdained by the nobility to which the *milites* belonged, who continued to base their social primacy on the art of war. The evolution of the order in the second half of the thirteenth century greatly enhanced the value of its commercial and financial activities and the status of those who performed them. These became positions of great power, but they were not accessible to knights, who lacked the necessary training. One such post was that of central treasurer, the administrator who resided in the Tower of the Temple in Paris and played a key role in the finances of the kingdom of France. Another was that of receiver of Champagne, who collected and reinvested the taxes of that wealthy county, which hosted the most important commercial fairs in the West. It was absolutely necessary that the receiver and the treasurer maintained good relationships with the French crown. The preceptor of France and the visitor general, who resided in Paris, were likewise bound to the crown. These dynamics were already in play at the time of King Louis IX, who did everything in his power to elect as preceptor of France a man close to himself, the knight Amaury de la Roche. Templar grand master Thomas Bérard protested against the king's efforts, reminding him that the Temple enjoyed full independence from the crown and that its members were not the servants of secular rulers. But in the end, the king got his way, convincing Pope Clement IV to intervene personally on behalf of his candidate.

In the final years of the thirteenth century, there were two poles of power within the Temple: one in Cyprus, composed primarily of soldiers still engaged in diplomatic dialogue with the Christian governments in the East to devise new plans for taking back the Holy Land, and one in the West, led by financier sergeants and knights with administrative and diplomatic posts for whom maintaining good relations with the rulers of Europe was the top priority.

Immediately following the death of Guillaume de Beaujeu, the grand master who had fallen in the heroic attempt to defend Acre, the Templars who had retreated to Cyprus held an emergency general chapter before electing a successor. At that meeting, a French knight named Jacques de Molay, who had had a brilliant career in the Temple, winning appointment to important posts shortly after joining the order, exhorted the leadership to take measures to eradicate certain immoral practices among the Templars before such indignities caused more serious problems. Molay had spent several years fighting at the front in the Holy Land, where veteran Templars had instructed him in the tactics of war and where he had distinguished himself with honor. He won the esteem of high-ranking Templars, including Beaujeu himself. After the death of Beaujeu's successor, Grand Master Thibaud Gaudin, who governed for just over one year, Molay was nominated as a candidate for grand master.

Hugh de Faure, a Templar who participated in the chapter, described what transpired at the turbulent election. Although some historians do not consider him reliable, Faure lived in the East and was an eyewitness to the events he recounted, some of which were fully corroborated by what took place in later years.

At the general chapter called to elect Gaudin's successor, two opposing coalitions emerged, one in favor of Molay and the other in support of a very prominent knight in the order, Hugh de Pérraud, grandson of the powerful Visitor of the Temple in France, Hubert de Pérraud. Hugh had had a thirty-year career in the Temple in the West, serving as commander of important houses and assuming diplomatic posts, including assignments to the papacy. Although Pérraud hailed from the ranks of knighthood, he had never been to the East and had never engaged in battle with the Muslim enemy. Pérraud enjoyed the support of the Templar leaders of the provinces of Auvergne and Limousin. Faure didn't specify which group supported Molay, but Molay's eminent military career suggests that his support came mostly from the Templars in the East, the veterans who had fought with Beaujeu.

After the death of Thibaud Gaudin, Jacques de Molay had assumed temporary command of the Temple with the title of grand commander, a sort of regency that many Templars believed was a prelude to his election as head of the order. Given his brilliant career, this rise to power is not surprising, but the defeat at Acre and the loss of the Christian kingdom in the Holy Land undermined his candidacy. Molay was the more authoritative and powerful of the two, but the French leaders supported a man who better represented them and their interests. The utter decimation of the Templars who had made the ultimate sacrifice at Acre put the Western contingent in the majority.

Hugh de Faure emphasized that the debates were hard fought. The Western faction wished to elect a diplomat and bureaucrat as the head of a military order created for the reconquest of the Holy Land. But how was he supposed to lead Templar forces in future crusading operations? To the Templars attending the chapter, the situation must have been very clear: choosing a man from the diplomatic corps as the grand master of the Temple spelled the inexorable decline of the order's military function.

The negotiations proceeded inconclusively until Jacques de Molay made it known that he would concede in favor of his opponent Hugh de Pérraud if the chapter officially confirmed his appointment to the post of grand commander. But once confirmed, Molay used his position to renegotiate the succession and skillfully maneuvered to become grand master, leaving to Pérraud the second most important post of visitor general.

What convinced the general chapter of the Temple, comprised mostly of Western Templars, to ratify Molay's election? Perhaps the answer lies in the compromise devised by Molay. Forced to return to the East to plan an imminent military operation, Molay issued a proxy granting Pérraud as visitor general the right to act as his plenipotentiary to assist the pope in case of need without having to wait for approval from Cyprus. Molay's proxy, which may have been the deal he proposed in order to win his election, reinforced the Temple's changing organizational structure. If the grand master, who was the military and political head of the order, had to reside primarily in the East to monitor events in the region and devise new plans for the reconquest of the Holy Land, the West needed to be guided by an administrator who would be responsible for the Temple's diplomatic relations with the European courts. Hugh de Pérraud, who had performed this task with papal approval over the course of thirty years of exceptional and honorable service, was decidedly the right man for the post.

The order's new diarchic structure was provisional, dictated by historical contingencies, and was meant to re-

vert to its original form with the recapture of the Holy
Land. This adaptation held up quite well until events
brought Molay and Pérraud — who by temperament and
background held diametrically opposed views regarding
the future of the order — into conflict.

Church and State

In his confrontation with the papacy, Philip the Fair had
the support of the French clergy in realizing his intention
of creating a Church of France independent of the Church
of Rome headed by Boniface VIII. When the king gathered the representatives of the French hierarchy at the
Louvre and drew up an indictment charging the pope with
heresy and unworthiness, among them was the Visitor of
the Temple in France, Hugh de Pérraud.

The Templar plenipotentiary did not put forward any
personal accusations against the pope, but Pérraud *did*
sign the warrant, probably because he was forced to do so
by the king. It was a very serious act. First, this radical pronouncement in favor of one of the parties to the conflict of
powers then in progress had been made without consult-
ing the grand master, who was in Cyprus at the time. Second, it seemed truly paradoxical that he should join in
proclaiming the illegitimacy of the same Boniface VIII on
whose behalf, just a few years earlier, the Templars had
covered a large expenditure, in the amount of 12,000 gold

florins, for the express purpose of defending his legitimacy. Finally, and this was the worst offense of all, his signature on the indictment betrayed one of the fundamental precepts of the Templar code of honor: absolute obedience and fidelity to the pope, who had raised them above other religious orders and showered them with exceptional privileges. Pérraud's act made the French leadership of the Templars appear independent of the central leadership of the order. It also made the Temple itself seem like a mercenary force, ready to change flags in the name of opportunity. Pérraud may have had little choice in the matter. Indeed, the visitor general asked the king to issue a curious document, a warrant of insurance that guaranteed Pérraud and his family the protection of the crown.

The incident at the Louvre passed unnoticed with no apparent damage to the Temple. The unexpected death of Boniface VIII in 1303 and the deft political skills of his successor, Benedict XI (1303–4), who immediately worked to restore the dialogue with the French monarchy, tempered the conflict. But Benedict ruled for only eight months. His death sparked a dispute at the conclave to elect a new pope between the Italian cardinals loyal to the memory of Boniface VIII and the French cardinals friendly to Philip IV. The quarrel lasted for a year, after which Cardinal Napoleone Orsini, leader of the French faction, engineered the election of a candidate who was acceptable to both parties. But the head of the Italian contingent, the elderly cardinal Matteo Rosso Orsini, refused to sign the election decree and abandoned the conclave. The new pope, the French-man Bertrand de Got, chose the name of Clement V (1305–14), but he did not celebrate his coronation until the death of Cardinal Matteo Rosso Orsini. Both Orsini cardinals belonged to one of Rome's oldest and most powerful noble families.

With Matteo Rosso Orsini gone, Clement V engaged in another diplomatic duel, this time with Philip the Fair over the site of the papal coronation. The pope, a native of Gascony, preferred Toulouse, but the king's choice was Lyon. In the late fall of 1305, after nearly six months of exhaustive negotiations, Clement V celebrated his papal coronation in Lyon in the presence of Philip IV. The outcome of this first battle of wills would characterize the relationship between the monarch and the pontiff for the remainder of their reigns. Elected in French territory, Clement V remained in France because of pressure from the crown. He intensified his predecessor's policy of détente toward the most powerful monarch in Europe.

Rumors had long been circulating in the secular world of strange secret rituals practiced by the Templars: forms of subjugation in which veterans humiliated new recruits by forcing them to demonstrate their reverence for their superiors — even to the point of kissing their buttocks. This gossip was widespread and had been compounded by other rumors, with even more sinister implications. At the papal coronation, the king informed Clement V of these disturbing rumors and asked him to investigate. As the months went by, the king's lawyers compiled evidence for their dossier against the Templars, details of which the sovereign did not fail to whisper into the papal ear.

Scandals in Paris

In 1306, hard pressed by the cost of the war against King Edward I and unable to rely on a stable system of taxation that ensured a regular influx of revenues, the French crown reduced the gold content of its currency by two-thirds. A revolt broke out in Paris, and Philip the Fair was forced to take refuge with his court in the bastion of the Tower of the Temple. Some submit that the king, upon physically seeing the treasure in the custody of the Templars, was overcome by avarice and began to obsess over how he might appropriate it for himself. In light of the historical sources, this hypothesis seems too simplistic and theatrical. Philip knew quite well the value of that fortune. In fact, his maneuvering for the acquisition of the Temple by the crown was ongoing. It is quite credible that, threatened by the crowd who wanted to lynch him and by his own financial troubles, the king realized that part of the Templars' holdings derived from the investment of money that belonged to the crown, that the order possessed huge amounts of wealth while the country was on the threshold of bankruptcy, and that it was only fair, therefore, to force the Temple to contribute to the resolution of the crisis.

Philip the Fair demanded from the Templar central treasurer, Jean de la Tour, some 300,000 gold florins, an enormous sum equal to the annual budget of the powerful maritime republics of Genoa or Venice. The king's request might seem understandable to a modern observer. But it must be recalled that a good part of the money safeguarded by the Templars belonged to private creditors, who had entrusted it to them because of their excellent reputation, and that an equally large portion belonged to the church and had been invested to finance a future crusade. In any case, the treasurer not only granted the king the huge loan unbeknownst to the grand master, he didn't even ask for a guarantee that the funds would be repaid.

According to the account of the chronicler known as the Templar of Tyre, Jacques de Molay returned from the East in early 1307 and, as required by Templar bylaws, checked the order's books of account. He noticed the enormous shortage resulting from the loan to the king and immediately ordered Jean de la Tour expelled from the Temple with an irrevocable disciplinary sanction. This re-action may seem harsh, but it was absolutely called for according to the Templar disciplinary code, which provided for expulsion from the Temple for the taking or conceal-ment of even a minimal amount, anything in excess of four dinars. But Jean de la Tour was no ordinary Templar. In the second half of the thirteenth century, his uncle had directed work on the construction of the imposing intramural for-tress in Paris, the very tower from which his mercantile family had taken its name. Up until his loan to Philip IV, the treasurer's management of the Temple's finances had been flawless. He enjoyed close ties with his clients, which is to say, with nearly all of the rulers throughout the Mediterranean basin. Jean de la Tour was a perfect example of the bourgeoisie who at one time had been relegated to the margins of the Temple hierarchy and who in recent decades had gained great power in the organization. And the treasurer could count on another advantage: the protection of Visitor General Hugh de Pérraud, whose authority had probably granted Philip the Fair the huge, anomalous loan.

The severity of Templar regulations regarding theft was known to all, even to the public, and constituted the principal basis of the great trust the world placed in the honesty of the institution. Jean de la Tour was certainly not ignorant of these precepts, just as he surely must have known that Templar bylaws reserved to the grand master the right to grant loans of large sums and the duty to conduct regular inspections of the Temple's accounts.

When the rebellion broke out on the streets of Paris, Visitor General Hugh de Pérraud was present in the Tower. The special proxy Molay had issued verbally to Pérraud in 1298 to help Boniface VIII against the attacks of the Colonna family had never been revoked. The treasurer, pressed by the request of the king of France, must have obtained the consent of his highest accessible superior, Hugh de Pérraud. If that was not the case, and Jean de la Tour willfully placed himself above the Templar bylaws, then it is a sure sign of the order's decline, which was much further along than was previously supposed, and proof that the Western leadership of the Temple considered itself independent of the general staff of the order.

After his expulsion, the treasurer behaved as though he had been punished unjustly and intended to make his case to the highest authorities. The king of France intervened on la Tour's behalf to ask for his reinstatement. In response to Molay's refusal, Philip the Fair asked Clement V to intercede personally with the grand master of the Temple.

According to the Templar rule, only the pope could request the revocation of a disciplinary procedure. This precept had been included in the thirteenth-century bylaws, according to which the pope could make use of this right only if strictly necessary for the good of the order. To mitigate the damage caused by the incident, Clement V requested the reinstatement of la Tour, who had the gall to deliver personally to Jacques de Molay the papal letter requesting his rehabilitation. The grand master was deeply offended. According to accounts, he became uncontrollably irate and threw Clement V's letter into the flames of his fireplace. Nevertheless, he reinstated the treasurer, in obedience to the pope's order.

The papal protection was extended to Pérraud, who Molay also held responsible for the incident. In fact, Clement V issued an extremely unusual directive, commanding that Hugh de Pérraud maintain his position as visitor general, as though to squelch any internal effort to remove him.

The wave of scandals that rocked the French leadership of the Templars from 1303 to 1306 marked an important moment in the development of the strategy against the order by the Council of France. The conflicts had clearly undermined Templar cohesion. More ominously, Nogaret and the others had concrete evidence of the French leaders' malleability, in contrast to the intransigence demonstrated by the grand master. Although Molay had refused the Temple's merger with the Hospital, which would have allowed the French crown to gain control over the new unified order, it was evident that the Temple was not invulnerable. On condition, naturally, that leverage was applied in the right places.

Disquieting Rumors

In March 1307, according to the account of the anonymous Templar of Tyre, Jacques de Molay returned to the West at the pope's summons. Clement V ordered Molay to provide the Curia with a written copy of the rule of the order. The rule of the Templars had enjoyed pontifical approval for more than two hundred years, so this request implies that the pope nurtured serious suspicions regarding the state of the order's internal regulations, which he intended to subject to close scrutiny. According to another dignitary present at the meeting, Clement V forwent the usual formalities and immediately demanded an explanation for the infamous rumor of the idol said to be secretly venerated in the Temple. The pontiff hailed from the military aristocracy, so he knew well the chivalric traditions concerning veterans and new recruits. He had given no weight to reports of scurrilous barracks antics between comrades in arms that were said to be common practice among the Templars. However, the king's insinuations that the warriors of God were undermining essential tenets of the faith had touched a more sensitive chord. The Templars were a religious order under the jurisdiction of the Church of Rome, on equal footing with other orders such as the Benedictines, the Franciscans, and the Dominicans. What if it were really true that the plague of heresy was secretly spreading among its members?

In the late spring of 1307, the royal strategy against the Templars accelerated at a feverish pace. While the king was defaming the order's most eminent members in the various royal courts of Europe, the lawyers who belonged to the Council of France were gathering the fruits of an operation launched in utmost secrecy several years before, when as many as twelve spies were charged to join the order and live peacefully among the Templars and collect any information that could be used against them.

By July 24 this systematic attempt to undermine the good reputation of the Templars among the highest levels of society had proved so successful that the pope could no longer ignore it; he resolved to write to Philip IV. The grand master of the Templars, indignant at the rumors the sovereign had been spreading, expressly requested the pope to open an inquest into the state of the Temple so as to demonstrate that the slanderous accusations were unfounded. The pope, the only earthly authority with the right to investigate the Templars, planned to hold this inquest as soon as possible. Given the complexity of the bureaucracy of the Roman Curia, this meant several months. The pope would have to name inspectors to conduct the investigation, visit Templar houses, and interrogate its leaders as well as members of lower rank.

At this point, Clement V, who by all accounts was a very intelligent man, made a serious tactical error. He informed the king that his physicians had prescribed a detoxifying cure involving thermal baths and purgatives and urged him, therefore, not to send his ambassadors before the middle of October when, having completed the treatments, the pope would be resuming his duties. Knowing that the pope would be inactive for nearly three months, the king's lawyers pounced on the opportunity to spring their trap. They hurriedly assembled the material gathered by their spies into a complex case for the prosecution. Despite being patently false, the accusations were so shocking, so scandalous, so explosive, that they made rational reflection difficult. By way of sophistry, generalization, and manipulation, the royal lawyers managed to transform every failing, every fault, every misdeed of the Templars, into crimes against the faith. They built an elaborate and dangerously persuasive case that struck at the Achilles' heel of the once invulnerable order.

Achilles' Heel

When Pope Innocent II embraced the creation of the Order of the Knights Templar, he bestowed a rare privilege on the order that exempted the Templars from the jurisdiction of bishops, archbishops, and even the College of Cardinals. They answered to the pope alone. In the early 1200s, however, the rapid acceptance of the Catharist heresy — which denied that Jesus was fully God and fully man — among members of the church led Pope Honorius III (1216–27) to extend the investigative power of the inquisitor for Tuscia to members of the three orders previously exempted by the pope for their proven loyalty: the Templars, the Hospitallers, and the Cistercians. The Templars were still at the height of their power, and no one ever could have imagined they would be victims of negative propaganda. But in these radically different historical conditions, the Catharist heresy was a precedent that could be used to pierce the formidable aura of invincibility that surrounded the order. The pope had never withdrawn the inquisitor's special privilege, and the jurists of Philip the Fair ably exploited it to present the pope with a terrible fait accompli.

The Inquisition was born in the early part of the thirteenth century to defend the orthodoxy of the faith from
heretical attacks, and it was governed by inflexible procedures. A simple accusation was enough to trigger an arrest
warrant, and the accused was immediately interrogated. If
he was believed to be lying, he was subjected to torture to
induce a confession. The inquisitor, however, needed the
secular power, the state, to execute the arrest warrants and
the torture. The governing authorities were obliged to
obey, and refusal — even displaying a lack of enthusiasm
in supporting the work of the tribunal — meant running
the risk of being labeled an accomplice to heresy. Suspicion
alone was so oppressive that many of the accused recanted
even though their guilt had not yet been demonstrated.
Not even informers were completely safe; if their accusations were later shown to be false, they risked heavy sanctions. Although the church launched the Inquisition with
purely defensive objectives, over time it was unable to effectively control it. As the Inquisition grew more complicated, it enjoyed greater autonomy. It became a mechanism
capable of swallowing everyone who had the misfortune
of falling into its grasp, a sort of quicksand from which it
was almost impossible to escape. The lawyers on the Council of France knew very well the tortuous ways of this complex machine of death, and they needed it to accomplish
the king's ends because *only* the inquisitor had the power
to breach Templar immunity.

At the end of the summer of 1307, while Clement V

was engaged in his detoxifying treatments, the men of Philip the Fair organized a secret meeting between the pope and Visitor General Pérraud, who Clement admired and had sent on diplomatic missions. The visitor general was responsible for supervising the order throughout the West and had the greatest experience in its initiation rites, given that he often presided at them. Pérraud confirmed to the pope that the Templars practiced a ritual that required new members to deny Christ and spit on the cross during their induction ceremony.

According to the royal strategy, this revelation should have been a mortal blow to the honor of the Temple, which Philip the Fair had already discredited in the royal courts of Europe and about which by now even the pope harbored some doubts. The lawyers for the crown probably believed that the encounter with Pérraud would force the pope either to issue a rapid condemnation of the order or proceed more quickly with his own inquest. They came away empty-handed on both counts.

Clement V was a canon lawyer with two university degrees who had worked for almost twenty years in the diplomatic corps of the Holy See before his election to the papacy. He had a reflective, stolid temperament, but he was also very astute, and he was evidently knowledgeable enough about the internal problems of the Templars to intuit that the visitor general's intentions went far beyond the mere desire to serve the truth. During a private discussion held in the royal castle of Loches, in the presence of

Philip the Fair and the prior of the Hospitallers of France, another Templar dignitary was on the verge of revealing to the king details concerning the secret ceremony in exchange for royal protection. The series of events involving high-ranking Templars in France reflected a Templar leadership deeply divided between its Eastern and Western factions, with the latter exhibiting much closer ties to the French crown.

On September 22, 1307, the inquisitor for France, the Dominican Guillaume de Paris, wrote a secret letter to his subordinates, the inquisitors for Toulouse and Carcassone, announcing that an arrest warrant was about to be issued against the Templars and urging them to prepare themselves for the inquest proceedings. The Dominican specified that the operation was not directed at the order as a whole but only at some individuals, about whom there were vehement suspicions of heresy. Undoubtedly, Guillaume de Paris had been informed of the royal strategy, the Council having voted in absolute secrecy on September 14 in favor of arresting the Templars, but the king had misrepresented the facts. In his letter, the inquisitor described the operation as though Philip the Fair was acting on orders from the pope. By emphasizing that the proceeding was aimed exclusively at certain persons, Guillaume de Paris kept himself solidly within the sphere of his own powers, which in accordance with the privilege issued by Honorius III could only be applied to specific individuals. The initial indictment targeted only Grand Master Jacques de Molay and a circle of his closest advisers. An inquest would eliminate this headstrong individual and pave the way for the succession of a more malleable candidate, someone like Visitor General Pérraud.

When the true intention and scope of the king's scheme became evident, the inquisitor protested vehemently to the king — to no avail. The visitor general then understood the gravity of his mistake, realizing that he had been used to strike a fatal blow against the Temple. Repenting his error, he tried to warn his brothers and exhort them to escape, but as he had isolated himself by his rivalry with Jacques de Molay, his appeal fell on deaf ears.

Whether or not Clement V realized it, the king's strategy had succeeded brilliantly: the visitor general of the Temple, a man who had participated in thousands of initiation ceremonies, had testified before the pope that the Templars engaged in a ritual in which novices were forced to deny Christ and spit on the cross. These were acts of repudiation of the faith, typical of heretics, and in cases of suspected heresy, the Inquisition's power extended even to members of the Temple. The crown misled Guillaume de Paris into believing that the inquest was ordered by the pope and would affect only some of the leaders of the order, and persuaded him to issue the indictment. It was not until dawn on October 13, 1307, when the king's men arrested and interrogated *all* the Templars in the realm, that the pope, the Templar visitor general, and the inquisitor for France all realized they had been masterfully outwitted.

VI

On Trial

"Will You Be Able to Bear the Unbearable?"

What were the immoral practices Jacques de Molay had denounced to the leadership at the meeting of the general chapter in Cyprus in 1291, and what harm would they cause the Temple if immediate action were not taken to eradicate them?

Studying the secret life of the Templars — their internal traditions cloaked by a rigid code of silence typical of a military order — is an arduous task for historians. Most of the sources pertain to their trial, which produced an abundance of tampered documents and testimony extracted under torture. It is a potential minefield, one that requires proceeding with great prudence. Nevertheless, it is extremely fertile and practically unexplored terrain.

In four years of research I produced a compendium of all Templar testimony over the course of the entire trial. This made it possible to compare the behavior of various brothers in identical situations and to verify if there were acts or omissions that were repeated systematically or if certain dignitaries customarily behaved in a manner different from others. I was able to juxtapose thousands and thousands of scattered pieces of information, which revealed that a number of secret rituals were regularly performed in the Temple, handed down by oral tradition and about which the written rule of the order contained nothing more than an imperceptible allusion. On the one hand, we have a wide range of information gathered from trial testimony, which provides clear evidence of certain recurrent practices, and on the other, the body of Templar rules and regulations preserved in original manuscripts written prior to 1291. The manuscripts allow us to draw some interesting comparisons, and they are above any suspicion of having been manipulated for purposes involving the trial since they date from the period when the order still enjoyed great power throughout Christendom.

When Bernard of Clairvaux delineated the rigid ethical and disciplinary code of the Templars, he was perfectly aware that this way of life would not be accessible to everyone. For this reason, he insisted on inserting into the text of the rule a clause exhorting the leaders of the order not to accept new vocations too hurriedly, but rather to subject candidates to a test to ascertain their character and commitment. The exact nature of the test is unclear. Bernard elegantly alluded to Saint Paul's advice to "put them to the test to see if they come from God." This referred to a training period, or novitiate, during which the aspirant lived with the Templars and shared their life in every aspect, experiencing combat against the Muslim enemy but also the harsh discipline of the order to confirm whether or not he could meet the severe demands of its code of honor.

A cardinal point of the Templars' ethical code was absolute obedience to one's immediate superiors, which was essential to the success of military operations. In a religious sense, absolute obedience meant a Templar must give up his free will and entrust himself completely to his superior, who was enlightened and guided by God.

The Templars' hierarchical statutes, which regulated the rules of engagement for combat, declared that the knights of the Temple could not abandon the battlefield even if they had been completely disarmed. The honor of the order required that they sacrifice their lives. We learn from a Muslim source that in 1188, as Saladin's army broke through the walls of the city of Darbsák, near Antioch, the Templars filled the breach with their own bodies, and as soon as one fell, another stepped in to take his place. Such a capacity for self-sacrifice required not only the strongest possible ideological commitment to the ethical code but also the proper psychological conditioning to prepare the knights for battle. Training them in the concept of absolute obedience was clearly a key element of their rigorous discipline.

The written statutes of the Temple, which date back to the second half of the thirteenth century, contain the complete text of the initiation ceremony. In the two centuries after the founding of the order, the moment at which a man gave up his secular life and took the religious vows to become a Templar had been rigidly codified, and both the leaders who officiated at the ritual and the postulant followed a precise script. The preceptor or commander of the Templar house where the ceremony was held, or alternatively a higher-ranking visiting dignitary who was invited to preside at the ceremony, examined the recruit three times to verify that he was fit for the Temple. Isolated in a separate room, the postulant was brought before the officiator, who showed him the rule of the Temple and warned him of its severity: "Sir, you see us well clothed and provided with the best horses, but very few know what our souls must withstand. If you become a Templar, you will have to face difficult challenges, hear outrageous words and accept them with patience, and obey your superiors no matter what they command you to do. Will you be able to bear the unbearable?"

The postulant responded, "Sir, with God's help, I can bear anything!"

The written rule offers no details as to how the preceptor might discourage postulants who were less than totally convincing, leaving it up to the discretion of whoever was presiding to do "as best he could and knew how." Then the candidate recited the three monastic vows of poverty, chastity, and obedience, removed his lay garments, and donned his religious dress. Once the preceptor fastened the clasp of the mantle of the Temple around the candidate's neck, he was a member of the order in all respects. This was the end of the ceremony as described in the written rule, but not of the actual ceremony, which included a part that can be reconstructed only from the testimony given at the trial.

All the Templars who testified at the trial recounted the first part of their induction exactly as it is described in the rule, with its liturgy, the interrogation, the vows, and the change of dress. After donning the mantle, the new Templar was led to an isolated place (in the sacristy, behind the altar, or in another room), and here the preceptor said: "Sir, all the vows you have made to us are empty words. Now you will have to prove yourself with deeds," and, without providing any explanation, the preceptor ordered the new Templar to deny Christ and spit on the cross, showing him a cross painted in a missal or using a liturgical cross. The novice Templar was often left speechless, and, having regained his senses after the shock, refused to obey. At that point the preceptor said: "You have sworn to obey any command from your superiors, and now you dare display your disobedience?"

A systematic analysis of all the testimony revealed that at this point most of the brothers resigned themselves to doing what had been commanded, perhaps attempting to spit in the direction of the cross without actually hitting it, while others adamantly refused. They had taken a vow to defend the faith and they would not soil themselves with such profanations. Sometimes a candidate's firmness was respected, and he was asked nothing more, but more often his brothers threatened him with prison or death, beating him brutally with their bare fists or holding a sword to his throat. Then the preceptor gave him the kiss of monastic brotherhood — on the mouth. Often this kiss, common to all religious orders, was followed by two more kisses on the belly and the posterior, which was usually covered by the tunic, but at times there were officiators who exposed their bottoms and, according to some witnesses, even obscenely proposed kisses on the penis. Most postulants obeyed without arguing when the request was moderately humiliating, such as a kiss on the behind, and refused in more extreme cases. While the preceptors demanded that a postulant at least deny Christ or spit on the cross, they usually overlooked a refusal of kisses, and unwilling candidates were not forced to comply.

Finally, the preceptor exhorted the new Templar not to have sexual relations with women, inviting him, should he absolutely not be able to live chastely, to unite with his brothers and not to refuse them should they request sexual favors from him. The novice often reacted angrily, but there were no consequences because the ritual sequence did not provide for any concrete application of this "precept of homosexuality." In practice, all the candidate had to do was submit to those words in silence with no signs of rebellion, as proof of his obedience.

The surviving trial testimony consists of approximately one thousand depositions with only six attesting to homosexual relations, all of which were described as long-term relationships that almost always had a dimension of affection. In the Temple, such relationships involved a small number of individuals. The practice of homosexuality was not widespread, not least because the rule punished such conduct with life imprisonment.

At the end of the ceremony, the "victim" of all these impositions was invited to report to the chaplain of the order to confess the sins he had just committed and ask for forgiveness. The priests of the Temple comforted these penitents by telling them that they had not committed grave offenses and that if they demonstrated remorse and shame, they would be absolved. Often, however, the brothers confessed to priests outside the Temple, generally Franciscans or Dominicans, who, naturally, were dumbfounded and amplified the brothers' moral disquiet by telling them they had committed mortal sins, sometimes encouraging them to leave the order. The indiscretions of these honest priests, who were totally ignorant of the real function of the secret ceremony within the Temple, undoubtedly contributed to the gossip circulating in the secular world about the "dark side" of the order.

The Secret Initiation Test

When the pope finally interrogated the Templars in person, he posed a series of questions aimed at clarifying the rumors that had led him to demand that Jacques de Molay provide him with a copy of the Templar rule. The problem, according to the pontiff, was that the rule itself was kept secret; the brothers learned its precepts only as they were instructed by their superiors. The extremely limited circulation of the Templar rule fostered misunderstandings and confusion between the official written law and the unofficial oral tradition, which was no less binding because the brothers' superiors required them to obey it. Clement V ascertained that none of the brothers who appeared before him had even so much as read a passage from the book of Templar bylaws, and even the preceptors responsible for entire Templar districts possessed only those extracts from the rule that applied to their specific duties, while the complete text was kept by the grand master and the group of wise men. The rest, therefore, had to believe what they were told.

During his inquest, the pope discovered that the initiation ritual had been observed by the Temple for at least one hundred years. But what did it mean? And more important, what was its purpose? The best informed opinion within the order about the function of this strange practice identified it as a test of courage and martial disposition. We know that the Saracens used to beat and torture captured Christians, forcing them to deny Christ and spit on the cross before ultimately compelling them to convert to Islam. Perhaps the true purpose of the ritual was to evaluate the new recruit's response to such an unexpected, shocking, and challenging situation. Commanded and even beaten to induce him to deny Christ just minutes after having embraced the religious life, the new Templar's instinctive reactions were probably what most interested the preceptors. This test stripped bare a man's true character, and it was at that point that courage, pride, determination, and the capacity for self-control emerged — all essential qualities for a Templar destined for combat operations and a career of command. By contrast, if what emerged was an attitude of timidity, an excessive readiness to obey, or, on the other hand, undue arrogance, the candidate was assigned to different duties. Indeed, when we examine the careers of last-generation Templars, we see that there were men, such as Jacques de Molay, who were sent immediately to the front lines in the Holy Land, and others, like Hugh de Pérraud, who were prized for their diplomatic and administrative skills, who served exclusively in the West.

The preceptors disdained the practice of the initiation ritual, but they considered it an obligation that had to be satisfied. Perhaps they accepted it because it immediately confronted the new Templar with the violence that he would be subjected to if he were captured by the Saracens, and anyone who had taken his vows lightly would learn very quickly the exacting way of life of the Templar. Furthermore, perhaps it tested the candidate's ability to abdicate his personal will in order to execute the commands of his superiors and served to teach absolute obedience, the true cardinal principle of Templar discipline. Interestingly, visiting dignitaries who were invited to officiate at initiation ceremonies almost always chose not to perform the ritual. Once the official ceremony provided for in the written rule had been completed, they tended to take their leave, entrusting to a subordinate the unpleasant chore of presiding over the second part.

Some novices were given preferential treatment. When the candidate for admission was known by the preceptor, he was given an abbreviated ceremony. An eloquent, if unusual, example of such favoritism is the case of Geoffrey de Gonneville, who was inducted into the order at the tender age of eleven at the request of his powerful aristocratic family, who had ties to the English monarchy. Accompanied by his noble parents, Geoffrey was entrusted to the care of the preceptor and underwent the second part of the ritual, just as adult candidates for admission. Although frightened when confronted with the demand to deny Jesus and spit on the cross, he retained his composure.

At that point, the boy refused and began to ask the whereabouts of his uncle and the other worthy persons who had accompanied him there; the preceptor told him, "They've gone away. And now you must obey me." But since the boy steadfastly refused, the preceptor, in the face of such determined resistance, made him a proposal: "I'll credit you with having done these things if you'll swear on the Gospels that you'll say that you did them to any Templar who may ask you!" The boy swore a solemn oath, and the preceptor excused him from doing all except this: having covered the cross with his hand, he ordered the boy to spit on his hand. When asked why he had been so indulgent to the boy, he answered that the boy himself and especially his uncle, who was a relative of the king of England, had done many favors for the preceptor of London in the past and had several times brought him to the royal apartments.

The ritual took place according to a fixed script based on the actual experiences of Templar escapees from Muslim prisons, and dated back to the earliest days of the order. It is reasonable to conclude that, at least in its essential aspects, such a rite of initiation had emerged from an interpretation of the brief passage in the rule that required the preceptors to ascertain the good faith of candidates. Over time, extraneous elements were added, such as the kiss on the buttocks, a true example of hazing, aimed at humiliating the recruit in front of the veterans, and the verbal exhortation to homosexuality, which probably started as a parody of the precept that required Templars to give their whole selves to the order and to their brethren. These vulgar and derisive practices were typical of the often crude behavior found among military corps, and probably arose when the order's traditional discipline began to deteriorate. According to a Templar source, this happened under the leadership of Grand Master Thomas Bérard, who oversaw the crucial twenty years of Templar defeats at the hands of the sultan Baibars. According to information in the pope's possession, however, these practices had already begun decades before.

One fundamental question centered on the ambiguous

nature of the entire ceremony. The new Templar was left to determine on his own what lesson he was meant to be learning, and neither the preceptor nor the brethren in general provided any explanation of the singular scene in which the candidate had been involved immediately following his induction. Only rarely did onlookers, unable to contain themselves, erupt in laughter and inform the new Templar that it was a practical joke. But there was nothing comic about the original version of the ritual. It was a trial of initiation to the challenging life of a Templar, which the new recruit was about to begin.

The last point raised in the indictment against the Templars concerned the secret veneration of an idol in the shape of a bearded male head. There is clear evidence of the existence of an unusual image of Christ in the religious life of the order, as well as a mysterious cult devoted to the Sacred Blood. On the feast of the Last Supper, the Templars celebrated a unique liturgical ceremony, perhaps derived from popular traditions in Jerusalem going back to the first centuries of the Christian era.

Fall 1307

Advised of the Templar arrests by a messenger while still undergoing his purifying treatments, Clement V immediately returned to the papal court in Poitiers and summoned all the cardinals for an emergency meeting to deal with the crisis. These were unprecedented events: the king of France, the head of a secular power, had arrogated to himself the right to decide questions of religious orthodoxy. Worse, he had laid his hands on a religious order, a part of the Church of Rome, which only the pope had the authority to judge.

Immediately following the arrest of the Templars, Guillaume de Nogaret gathered a crowd in the gardens of the royal palace in Paris and publicly proclaimed the charges against the order: at the moment of initiation, new brothers were forced to deny Christ, spit on the cross, kiss the preceptor on the mouth, the belly, and the buttocks, and ordered not to deny themselves carnally to their brethren who might wish to unite with them. The final charge was the alleged existence of an idol in the form of a male head with a long beard that the Templars were said to worship in secret and to which they girded themselves with a cord consecrated by physical contact with the idol.

Philip IV implemented his strategy of surprise for the same reason that Grand Master Jacques de Molay had asked the pope to open an investigation of the Temple: to exercise some control over the procedure in the hope of determining its outcome. A papal inquest would have been a legitimate investigation, carried out in full respect of canon law entirely within the church. Its aim would have been to rid the order of its shortcomings and promote its reform. But it was precisely the reconstruction of the order that the king wished to avoid at all costs. Arrested without warning, subjected immediately to indiscriminate torture to obtain confessions of guilt, the Templars were exposed to public opinion of the time. The warriors of God, who had sworn to give their lives to defend the faith, had been corrupted to the point of denying Jesus, spitting on the cross, committing acts of depravation, worshipping an idol, and other untold nefarious deeds.

On October 25 the king organized a public hearing during which the grand master of the Templars had confessed that he was obliged to deny Jesus and spit on the cross during his own induction ceremony — scandalizing everyone present who knew nothing of Templar practices, much less their purposes. The king's lawyers involved the theologians of the Sorbonne in the trial of the Templars, enlisting their religious authority in support of the secular power of the monarchy, thereby creating a competing authority to the papacy. But within a few months, the theologians realized what the crown was attempting and took a more cautious position in line with the pope's orientation.

Confession before the theologians was an important step in the strategy of the prosecution. At the hearing, Guillaume de Nogaret announced the existence of a written confession signed by Jacques de Molay in which the grand master, appealing to their vow of sacred obedience, ordered all Templars to confess the acts committed in secret during their induction ceremonies. The letter, which was sent to Templar houses in France, was largely responsible, together with torture, for the enormous number of confessions during the fall of 1307. It was probably a counterfeit document created during an irregular deposition and then affixed with what looked to be the silver seal of the grand master of the Temple. But although it was trumpeted about as devastating proof, the letter was never delivered to the pope, perhaps because the notaries of the apostolic chancery had great experience in examining suspicious documents. The only one who had any direct involvement in Molay's confession was Guillaume de Nogaret.

Clement V, however, was forced to moderate his response because a significant number of the cardinals in the Sacred College looked favorably on the scheme of the French king. He drafted a letter of protest to Philip the Fair, carefully calibrated in its expressions of condemnation to enable the king to step away from his position without having to make a solemn apology to the pope. The excessively mild tone of the bull *Ad preclaras*, which ordered Philip the Fair to immediately release the Templars to the custody of the church, made the whole incident seem like an error in good faith committed by someone who had no knowledge of certain provisions of canon law.

To advise him on the matter, the pope wisely chose two men who were highly regarded by the king: Cardinal

Bérenger Frédol, Clement V's nephew and an expert in canon law, and Cardinal Etienne de Suisy, who had held the post of vice chancellor to the crown. Able diplomats, the two had the necessary experience to ascertain the truth about the thorny questions posed by this unsavory case. Frédol was well versed in the mechanisms of the Inquisition because he had conducted for the pope a careful investigation on the abuses of the tribunal for southern France, while Suisy knew the men and the environment of the Council of France quite well.

When they arrived in Paris, the two papal legates were stonewalled. Rather than take them to the Templars, the royal councillors introduced them only to the theologians of the Sorbonne who had heard the depositions of the grand master and who recounted these for them. The two cardinals were forced to return to Poitiers in early November without having seen the prisoners. The news of their fruitless mission set off a rebellion in the College of Cardinals. Some cardinals were said to have presented their resignations to the pope on the grounds that Clement V had not conducted himself as a pope but rather as a simple puppet in the hands of the king. These men were among the first that Clement V himself had appointed as cardinals: men of his own choosing, among them several of his own nephews, whom the pope had intended to be his closest advisers and who were now openly exhibiting dissent.

The College of Cardinals was deeply divided between those who demanded an explicit censure of the king —

who, seemingly ignorant of the provisions of the bull, had disobeyed the papal orders — and those who refused to tolerate a condemnation of the king. Clement knew that whatever decision he made would be challenged by one group; inherent in this was the risk that the discontented faction would declare its secession and proceed to elect a rival pope.

Papal custody of the men and property of the Temple was crucial. Indeed, not long after the arrest of the Templars in France, King James II of Aragon had begun speculating about the property of the order in his realm, to the point of asking the pope to grant him a donation or two from the Templars' sequestered estates should they be found guilty. Clement V was compelled to issue a bull on November 22, mandating that Templar property throughout Christendom fell under papal custody, in order to halt the pillaging of their estates.

Impassive but also astute, the pontiff decided to send his legates anew with the same objective. This time, however, Bérenger Frédol and Etienne de Suisy were given the authority, should they again be prevented from seeing the Templars, to excommunicate Philip the Fair and to put the kingdom of France under interdict, a punishment by which the faithful were forbidden from participating in the sacraments and other sacred acts.

Molay's Retraction and the Struggle over the Papal Investigation

On December 27, 1307, Grand Master of the Temple Jacques de Molay finally testified before the two papal envoys. He retracted his earlier confession, declaring that it had been extracted under torture. According to a contemporary account, Molay had asked to testify in public before an audience gathered in the cathedral of Notre Dame, where he removed his clothing to show the torture marks that had been inflicted on him. Another reported that Molay organized a resistance movement against the maneuvers of the prosecution, sending to all the cells where the Templars were held prisoner wax tablets informing them that the cardinals were on the way and encouraging them to revoke their earlier statements. The pope had forbidden the legates from proceeding with their interrogations of the Templars as long as they remained in royal custody; they were to proceed with their mission only when they were certain that they could work without the crown's interference.

We cannot say with any certainty whether there were contacts between the prisoners and the cardinals before the retractions, but the evidence indicates that the Templar "counterattack" had been prearranged. Some historians suspect that Molay's deposition in Notre Dame was the fruit of invention. While there may be legitimate doubts about the details of his testimony, there is no doubt about its impact.

Toward the end of January, immediately following the return of the two legates to Poitiers and their report on what had happened in Paris, the pope suspended the powers of the Inquisition in France, blocking all proceedings against the Templars that had been authorized by the decree issued several months earlier by Guillaume de Paris. The pope's position was crystal clear. Certain by now of the bad faith underlying the conduct of the trial, he wanted to interrogate the Templars in person, and he demanded that Phillip IV turn over the prisoners to the custody of the church.

Throughout the spring of 1308, a bitterly fought political battle raged between the pope, who refused to restore the powers of the Inquisition until he could interrogate the Templars directly, and the lawyers for the king of France, who delivered inflammatory speeches. They threatened to repeat the events involving Boniface VIII at Anagni and accused Clement V of wishing to promote the heresy of the Temple. The king's men circulated a series of defamatory pamphlets, the most interesting of which contested the pope's decision to suspend the trial on grounds that the grand master's confession had been extracted by torture — proving that the king had been forced to justify himself regarding Molay's physical appearance at Notre Dame. Then they published allegations against the pope of nepotism and even of an illicit affair with Countess Brunissenda of Périgord. This latter charge failed to achieve the desired effect because the lovely lady did not reside at the papal court. Finally, they issued warnings against Clement V's nephews.

The king's lawyers invoked the aid of the Sorbonne theologians, inviting them to testify to the king's behavior and to find arguments in support of his good faith. But the theologians, well aware of what was at stake, limited themselves to declaring that the king had acted in good faith, while upholding the pope's exclusive right to judge the Templars.

In June 1308, after months of conflict, the king of France gave in to the pope, realizing that his adversary would be able to keep the trial at a standstill indefinitely. He decided to send the pope a select group of Templar prisoners, as well as a few excommunicated fugitives from justice, so as to make the worst possible impression. The convoy, comprised of about seventy prisoners, transported in wagons and tied to each other at their hands and feet, also included key members of the general staff: the grand master, the visitors of the East and West, the preceptor of Normandy, and the preceptor of the provinces of Aquitaine and Poitou. However, with only three-quarters of the journey complete, the caravan suddenly split up, and the wagon with the highest-ranking leaders ended its journey at the fortress of Chinon on the Loire River instead of the papal court at Poitiers.

The king and his strategists justified this with the pretext that the Templar leaders were sick and unable to continue the journey. It was a deft attempt to sabotage the validity of the papal inquiry. If Clement V pronounced a verdict favorable to the Templars, as the king evidently believed he would, it would carry very little weight without the testimony of the leaders of the order. The Templars Philip sent to the pope were mostly sergeants and low-ranking officers who were not morally or materially representative of the order. The king's plan, or more precisely, the plan of the lawyers to whom Philip the Fair had for all practical purposes delegated the conduct of the trial, was based on a series of clever expedients designed to block any move by the pope without ever entering into direct conflict with him. After a year of vexation, subterfuge, and diplomatic skirmishes, the pope was finally able to see the Templars personally, even if the group was without its leaders.

From June 28 to July 2, 1308, Clement V and a commission of cardinals conducted the Roman Curia's inquest into the Templars. The original documents, almost all of which have been preserved, demonstrate that it was an honest proceeding, conducted in full respect of the law, without any form of pressure exerted on the defendants. On the contrary, the Templars were invited to denounce the mistreatment they had been subjected to at the hands of the French king in order to clarify how much of their previous declarations could be attributed to torture.

The inquest was recorded exclusively by papal notaries,

who verified each other's documents in order to prevent copying errors from altering the facts. Likewise, the choice of cardinals to sit on the commission had been made with an eye toward maintaining an ideological balance. The pope insisted on having his two veterans of the dispute, his nephew Bérenger Frédol and Etienne de Suisy. They were joined by two Francophiles who were nonetheless loyal to the church and fair, the Neapolitan Landolfo Brancacci and the Frenchman Pierre de la Chapelle-Taillefer, and lastly, by a man who had been publicly compromised: Pietro Colonna. One of Boniface VIII's enemies, Colonna had been excommunicated and readmitted as part of the negotiations that restored diplomatic relations between France and the Vatican. Colonna was probably appointed only to ensure that the commission reflected all of the positions present in the College of Cardinals.

Clement V personally presided over the interrogations. As the depositions proceeded, he relied on a series of well-crafted questions to delve into how the abusive practices came to spread throughout the order. At the conclusion of the inquest, the pope understood that the strange custom perpetuated by the order as a compulsory test required new Templars to deny Christ and spit on the cross. Although it was an unworthy tradition that the Templars had further embellished with other vulgar and violent practices, under no circumstances could it be confused with heresy, an offense that implied a strict and long-term adherence to subversive doctrines.

The Templars' crime, therefore, was tolerating the development of this shameful ritual and failing to eradicate it or denounce it to the higher authority of the pope. The trial also brought to light some other offenses, such as abuses of power, theft, and less serious deeds, which certainly did not rise to the level of heresy but which nevertheless compromised the honor of the order. Although he had fought hard to conduct his own inquest, Clement V had no intention of being indulgent toward the flaws of the Temple. He shared the view of his predecessors, who at least as far back as the Council of Lyon (1274) had believed that the military orders were in crisis and were in need of radical reform. The pope's objective was to force the Templars, who had always been opposed to a merger with the Hospitallers, to acknowledge their failings and responsibilities and to realize that the survival of the order was dependent on its transformation. Clement V wanted to limit the damage done by the defamation orchestrated by the king of France and to create ideal and practical conditions for the institution of a new unified order. The pope ordered the Templars to ask for forgiveness, then absolved them from the excommunication that they had brought upon themselves and restored them to full membership in the Catholic community. Clement V was working toward reforming the Temple by providing the order with a new rule. His interest in the text of the Templar rule may be evinced both from the testimony and from the questions he addressed to the Templars at the inquest. The legal and moral reintegration of the Templars into the Catholic community, guaranteed by the pope's absolution, was the indispensable precondition for their absorption into a new order.

The Chinon Parchment

On July 10, 1308, the pontiff repeated the collective absolution of the penitent Templars in the house of Cardinal Pierre de la Chapelle, whom he had appointed as their official guardian five days earlier. Philip the Fair was in Poitiers at the time and remained there for another ten days. On July 20 he returned to Paris, leaving his trusted lawyer, Guillaume de Plaisians, at the papal palace to monitor events and safeguard the crown's interests. Clement V had absolved the Templars who had appeared before him, but who were still detained and guarded by the king's soldiers, and he seemed resigned to the absence of the Templar leaders still imprisoned in the fortress of Chinon. On August 12, Clement V convened the College of Cardinals to give a public reading of a bull entitled *Faciens misericordiam* (*Granting Forgiveness*), which he had written four days earlier. The bull issued the call for a great ecumenical council to take place two years later to discuss the most urgent problems facing Christianity, including the organization of a new crusade, which Clement strongly supported,

and the question of the Templars. In preparation for the
council, the bull required inquests to be held throughout
Christendom, so that depositions of the defendants could
be gathered and transmitted to the pope, who would decide the fate of the order. During the council, the pope
would issue his verdict on the Templar leadership, who
would remain under his exclusive authority and who no
one would be allowed to question until that time.

The next day Clement V decreed the start of the summer holidays, which interrupted the political and legal activities of the Curia, and retired to the countryside. In all
probability, the representatives tasked by Philip the Fair to
watch over his interests at the papal court also left Poitiers
for Paris. All seemed calm. At the first light of dawn, cardinals Bérenger Frédol, Etienne de Suisy, and Landolfo
Brancacci left Poitiers and went directly to Chinon, not
stopping along the way even for the Feast of the Assumption (which celebrates the assumption of Mary into heaven,
body and soul) on August 15, one of the most important
holy days of the liturgical calendar. The pope had secretly
appointed them as his plenipotentiaries to hold the inquest
of the grand master and the other leaders of the Temple in
his stead. Interestingly, Cardinal la Chapelle, official custo-
dian and legal guardian of the Templars on behalf of the
church, was not part of the commission. So, while the
pope and the official legal delegate for the Templars were
almost certainly under strict surveillance, cardinals Frédol,

Suisy, and Brancacci had no problems making their way unnoticed. The zealous and savvy Jean Bourgogne, whom the king of Aragon had placed at the papal court for the sole purpose of gathering firsthand news, managed to learn of the cardinals' departure only six days after they had left — by which time they had already accomplished the mission entrusted to them by the pope.

At Chinon, the three cardinals met the members of the general staff and informed them of the situation — including the pope's intention to remove the disgrace of the trial by reforming the order and to unify the Temple and the Hospital, which he thought was vital to the success of a new crusade. The Templars' legal situation had been gravely compromised. Although it was clear that they were not heretics, it was equally clear that under church doctrine they were guilty, albeit of a much lesser offense. According to canon law, anyone who commits an act of rejection of the faith, even if he does so without conviction, removes himself from the Catholic community, effectively excommunicating himself. The excommunicant can be absolved of his guilt but cannot be acquitted. The circumstances very closely paralleled the case of apostates, those who had renounced their faith during periods of pagan persecution of the Christians in order to escape martyrdom. Even though their renunciation was a form of self-defense, those apostate Christians were nevertheless guilty and estranged from the community of believers. The fathers of the church sanctioned a severe sentence: those who committed the sin of apostasy could be absolved, but only if they solemnly requested forgiveness and accepted the penance imposed on them. The Templars, therefore, had to do the same. The pope was bound by a thousand years of church doctrine that not even he, despite holding the office of the sovereign pontiff, could contradict. The survival of the order could be assured only by the Templars' plea for forgiveness and acceptance of the penance, which in all likelihood would take the form of a merger with the Hospital.

The original record of this inquest held behind closed doors in the dungeon of Chinon, called the Chinon Parchment, documented the absolution of the Templar leaders and their full reintegration into the Catholic community. The record demonstrated that Jacques de Molay was in profound conflict with Hugh de Pérraud, that there were intensive negotiations, and that finally, the Templar grand master agreed to the pope's proposal.

On August 20, 1308, the Chinon inquest came to an end. Upon the return of the three cardinals to Poitiers, the pope drafted a second version of his bull *Faciens misericordiam*. It reiterated the main points expressed in the first release, but added that the leaders of the Temple had been absolved and were now protected by judicial immunity and that no one, except the Roman pontiff, could so much as interrogate them. With the issuance of the first bull,

Clement V had led the king's agents to believe that the Templar question would not be resolved for another two years. The pope's clever use of his three plenipotentiaries to absolve the Templar leaders and his release of the second bull ensured that any move by the king would come too late.

Either the Temple or the Church of Rome

The Chinon inquest may have been Clement V's way of retaliating against Philip the Fair for the blow the king had dealt him the year before — when the pope returned from his summer holiday ready to initiate the church's inquest into the Templars, only to find that his defendants had already been arrested, interrogated, and pronounced guilty. But the success of Clement's maneuver was short-lived.

The king's plan to put Boniface VIII on trial had not expired with Boniface's death: the pope's physical end did not nullify the sanctions he had placed against Philip the Fair, including the king's excommunication set forth in the bull *Super Petri solio*, which had never been published. The bull had been issued by Boniface in full possession of his powers, and that document, though never promulgated, threatened to undermine the legitimacy of the French crown. Furthermore, there were other documents issued by the pope against Philip the Fair during the most bitter moments of their conflict, such as the bull *Ausculta filii*

(*Listen, My Son*), and *Unam sanctam* (*The One Holy*), which declared the impossibility of eternal salvation for those outside of the Roman Church, a condition that Philip the Fair was dangerously approaching.

Clement V had drawn on his long legal and diplomatic experience to devise a brilliant stratagem for reducing the tension between the papacy and the crown: he erased from the sumptuous registries of Boniface VIII all of the harshest passages against the king. Having eliminated the material evidence of the conflict, Clement V put to rest Philip the Fair's challenges to the legitimacy of Boniface VIII's pontificate. But the Templar affair and Clement V's surprise move at Chinon provoked the king's lawyers to resurrect the issue and use it as a bargaining chip.

Philip IV made a formal request to convene a trial of the deceased Boniface VIII, relying on a terrible precedent that took place during one of the darkest periods in the history of the papacy, the Cadaver Synod. It involved Formosus, a cleric with a complex and highly controversial ecclesiastical career. In the year 864, Formosus became bishop of Porto in Portugal. During his term, he distinguished himself for his outstanding political and diplomatic skills. But a rival faction impeded his career, boycotting his candidacy for patriarch of Bulgaria, because at the time canon law prohibited a bishop from moving from one diocese to another. Compromised by his involvement in the plots of a high-ranking official in the papal court, Formosus committed the error of fleeing, appearing guilty even in the eyes of his defenders, and he was excommunicated. In 878, at a synod in Troyes, he threw himself at the feet of Pope John VIII, who absolved him after Formosus took an oath never to return to Rome and never to try to regain his old diocese of Porto. John VIII was succeeded by Marinus I, whose election nullified the effect of the provision of canon law that had been used to bar Formosus's appointment as patriarch of Bulgaria. Marinus I absolved Formosus and restored his bishop's chair in Porto.

In the year 891, Formosus was elected pope. Perhaps his only error as pope was allowing himself to be compromised by favoring the German king, Arnulf of Carinthia, in his struggle against the dukes of Spoleto for the crown of the Holy Roman Empire. In 895, Arnulf came to Rome, where Formosus crowned him emperor in a solemn ceremony. Arnulf died soon thereafter, followed shortly by Formosus himself, who was buried in the Basilica of Saint Peter, alongside his predecessors. The election of Pope Stephen VI, a member of the Spoleto faction, hostile to Formosus and the Germans, made possible the politically motivated Cadaver Synod. The new pope ordered the body of Formosus, which had been lying in his tomb for several months, exhumed, dressed in his papal garb, propped up on a chair, and made to answer for the pope's sins. In a grotesque, macabre, posthumous trial, Formosus, through the voice of a terrified young deacon, acknowledged his guilt. Pope Formosus's cadaver was mutilated of his tongue and the three fingers of his right hand, which he had used to impart benedictions. His body was thrown into the Tiber River, but was later retrieved by a compassionate monk. Stephen VI used the synod to declare Formosus's papacy, as well as all his acts as pope, illegitimate, therefore invalidating the coronation of Arnulf as Holy Roman Emperor.

Philip the Fair wished to enact a similar theatrical drama against the memory of the deceased Boniface VIII, except that the pope's cadaver, buried for five years, was presumed to be reduced to bones. The king's men threatened to exhume the bones of Pope Boniface VIII for a trial that would declare him a heretic, a blasphemer, an atheist, and a practitioner of witchcraft, and order his remains to be burned at the stake in the manner reserved for the enemies of the faith.

The charges the king intended to bring against the apostolic authority were much greater than that of its precedent. Formosus had been tried for violating the canonical prohibition against moving from one bishopric to another; there had been no allegations of immorality. In this case, a secular power would accuse Boniface VIII of quintessentially religious crimes, as though to declare that the king of France was better qualified as a guarantor of the faith than the miscreant pope. The spectacle of burning Boniface VIII's bones would serve only to emphasize a complete reversal of institutional power relationships. It would impress on the public consciousness that this was the beginning of a new era in which the secular power of the French monarchy would lead Christian society — if necessary as an alternative to the papacy, which was believed to have reached such a state of decadence as to be incapable of performing its traditional role. While the Council of France drafted a program for the complete reform of the structure of the church, the bishops of the realm gathered to express their loyalty to the king, in support of his plan to create an independent Church of France, separate from Rome.

In October 1308, Bishop Guichard of Troyes was accused of witchcraft and burned at the stake, despite having been acquitted by the pope. This act was Philip the Fair's attempt to further illustrate that the whole Roman Church was rotten with heresy, since a pope, a bishop, and even an entire religious order had foundered on the shoals of corruption. A few months later, Cardinal Napoleone Orsini wrote to inform the king that he had found witnesses of the utmost authority in Italy who would prove the guilt of Boniface VIII and that he was ready to bring them to France to testify at the trial.

Clement V's conflict with Philip IV promised to be a reprise of the dispute that had consumed Boniface VIII in his time, with the prospect, given the imbalance of power, of the church suffering a ruinous defeat in its effort to achieve the legal survival of the Temple — an order that had been irreparably damaged. Most of the Templars who had not died in prison or from the torture inflicted by the king's soldiers were exhausted and debilitated by the infamy that had been hurled against them. Clement V, weakened by the illness that had afflicted him for years and outmaneuvered by the king, surrendered the fight and abandoned the Order of the Knights Templar to its fate. As head of the Roman Church, the pope's immediate responsibility was the preservation of the institution, which Philip the Fair threatened to splinter. It was a practical calculation.

In August 1309, Clement V wrote a letter to all bishops throughout Christendom. Most, except those in France, had yet to initiate a single proceeding against the Templars, even though almost a year had passed since they had been charged to conduct such inquests. The letter explained, "to those of you who may be expecting the pope to draft a new order for the Templars," that this was no longer going to happen, and exhorted them not to delay their inquests any further. However, most bishops were convinced that Clement V intended to save the Temple and reform it. This was a reasonable conclusion, considering that the original bull sent to the bishops ordering the inquests was entitled *Granting Forgiveness*, and no document with such a name could have contained a decree of condemnation. Accounts written by people in and around Clement's court, expressed the identical belief that the pope was working to ensure the survival of the Temple. This generally shared opinion explains the behavior of several prelates of the time, such as Rinaldo di Concorezzo, archbishop of Ravenna, who absolved the Templars in his diocese for insufficient evidence, and Peter of Mainz, who had a detailed inventory of all the goods possessed by the order drawn up so as to be able to restore these to the Temple once it had been rehabilitated.

Contrary to what his bishops believed, Clement V had chosen in good conscience what seemed to be the lesser evil. He had sacrificed the Temple to save the unity of the church.

From the Council of Vienne to the Death of Jacques de Molay

Between the end of 1309 and the first few months of 1310, the diocesan inquests that Clement V had called for in the summer of 1308 finally began. On July 5 the pope restored to the Inquisition its judicial powers while specifying that the inquests be handled by the local bishops and that the tribunal would participate only in a marginal way, should it insist on doing so. This substantial dismissal of the body authorized to investigate crimes of heresy can be attributed to the fact that the pontiff was clearly convinced that the Templars were not guilty of heresy and by the abuses committed by the Inquisition in supporting the challenge of the king of France to the primacy of the church.

The accounts of the various inquests were notarized and sent to the Curia, where officials of the chancery supervised the compilation of an ample dossier. The tenor of the proceedings reflected the political orientation of the individual bishops. In France and the areas subject to French influence, there continued to be rampant abuses, brutal torture, and intentional obfuscations, while in areas free of French influence, the documents revealed a greater respect for the rule of law. Philip IV did everything in his power to destroy the order. In 1310 he ordered fifty-four Templars who had been found innocent burned at the stake, in total violation of papal authority. Even the theologians of the Sorbonne opposed this decision, declaring it completely illegal, but their opinion was ignored.

In the south of France, where the powers of the Inquisition were strongest, there were records of convictions for violations associated with witchcraft, such as the witch's Sabbath and group orgies, which even went beyond the accusations of Philip the Fair in his indictment. The most baseless charges, which drew from the most abominable fantasies of the popular imagination, were brought against the Templars. However, from Cyprus, where the order had its headquarters, came heroic and mystical testimonies. There, the defendants included knights who had fought in the desperate defense of Acre in 1291 and whose depositions recalled both the military valor and the private faith of their brethren, especially that of the illustrious grand master Guillaume de Beaujeu, whose acts of beneficence were well known. There was also the testimony of a knight charged with guarding the Templar prisoners in their house, who had witnessed a eucharistic miracle during the daily Mass celebrated by the chaplain of the order. When the Templar priest raised the host at the moment of consecration, it became enormous and bright as sunlit snow, so bright that his eyes were dazzled.

The arrival of all this documentation in Poitiers in 1311 brought Clement V face to face with his painful dilemma. For the previous two years, he had relieved himself of responsibility for the trial by leaving the conduct of the inquests in the hands of individual bishops. He felt the immense weight of his moral burden and held out some hope of ensuring the survival of the Temple, which evidently he had never given up in his heart. During the long hearing that was held in Paris from 1310 to 1311, many Templars had proven their courage and their desire to remain faithful to their vows. More than five hundred presented themselves to the various bishop commissioners to testify in defense of the order.

Clement V and his advisers retreated to the abbey of Maucéne, where they spent weeks examining the enormous dossier of trial records. The pope had a summary of the evidence prepared, which he marked with his own notes. The results of this review were brought to the Council of Vienne, which opened on October 16, 1311, in the presence and under the military protection of the king of France.

On March 22, 1312, although the trial records did

not contain proof of the charge of heresy, Clement V issued the bull *Vox in excelso* (*A Voice from On High*), which dissolved the Order of the Knights Templar. The pope never issued a judgment of condemnation against the Templars. The suppression was justified not by canon law but by the necessity of avoiding irreparable harm to the church. Former Templars were allowed to join other religious orders, including the Hospital, if they desired. In the bull *Ad providam*, Clement ordered all the property of the order transferred to the Hospital out of respect for the original intention of the Temple's benefactors, who had made the donations to support the crusades.

Although the leaders of the Temple were still detained illegally by Philip IV, the pope granted them judicial immunity. Clement V was hoping to guarantee their safety by arranging for them to be kept under house arrest in the custody of the church. Templar grand master Jacques de Molay tried multiple times to obtain an audience with the pope, but royal agents prevented that meeting from ever taking place. Nor were the Templars allowed to be in contact with their grand master. Some organized a courageous resistance, uniting behind their chaplain Pietro da Bologna, a fine jurist, who openly denounced the lack of due process at the trial. The Templar chaplain succeeded in creating grave embarrassment for the representatives of the crown, but he swiftly disappeared in the royal prison. The others, who were practically illiterate, gave up the fight.

The situation remained unchanged at the beginning of 1314. The king aggressively pushed Clement V for a decision on the fate of the leaders, since only the pope could issue a final judgment on their case. The Templar leaders still posed a threat because the pope had absolved them of all charges and reconciled them with the Catholic community. Molay had even managed to obtain the services of a personal chaplain who celebrated Mass and the liturgical office in the grand master's cell every day.

Meanwhile, Clement V's illness had become terminal. For years he had been suffering from violent hemorrhages that forced him to take to his bed for days at a time; on several occasions he was thought to be close to death. Physically unable to deal with the question, Clement V named a commission of bishops to decide on the fate of the Templar leaders. In reality, the decision had already been made. All that remained was to implement the decree of perpetual detention in the custody of the church, a move that would ensure the safety of the leaders' lives and assure the king of France that the order would never be reconstituted.

Upon hearing the verdict of life imprisonment, Grand Master Jacques de Molay and his most trusted comrade, Preceptor of Normandy Geoffrey de Charny, refused to accept the sentence, proclaiming the Temple's absolute innocence of all the charges brought against them. The bishops on the commission adjourned the hearing to consult the pope. With the compromise solution uncertain, the king's fear was that the pope would overturn his recent acts or decisions concerning the Templars. Philip IV chose a drastic course of action that put an end to the Templar question once and for all. On March 18, 1314, the king had Jacques de Molay and Geoffrey de Charny seized from the legitimate custody of the commission and burned at the stake on an island in the river Seine.

Accounts of the execution attested to the great heroism demonstrated by the two leaders. Jacques de Molay asked his executioners to untie the knots around his wrists, raised his eyes to the cathedral of Notre Dame, and prayed to the Virgin Mary to whom Bernard of Clairvaux had dedicated the order. The Templars used to say that the order had started in the name of the Mother of God and it would end in the same way. With his prayer, the grand master bore glorious witness to the demise of the Temple and proclaimed its innocence and fidelity to the Christian faith.

The throng of onlookers rose in tumult, and the fires could not be lit until part of the crowd was dispersed. According to the poet Geoffroy de Paris, who was probably present at the execution, Jacques de Molay called before the judgment of God both the king of France, who had attacked the order without warning, and the pope, who had abandoned them. Clement V died on April 20, little more than a month after the execution. Apparently, even on his death bed the pope could not forgive himself for the miserable end of the Templars. Philip the Fair followed him several months later, on November 29. The fact that both died within a year after being summoned by the dying grand master to answer for their sins before God gave birth to legends of a curse, which persisted through the centuries. Seven hundred years after the fall of one of the medieval world's most powerful and charismatic institutions, the story of the Templars is still incredibly alive.

Afterword

There is much about the Templars that remains to be discovered. Research has given us new and exciting paths of investigation. This includes a special rite of the Passion of Christ celebrated on the evening of Holy Thursday, in commemoration of the Last Supper, in which the Templars probably received communion only in the form of wine, or the holy blood of Christ, the drink of eternal life. This highly unusual ceremony has captured the attention of a number of specialists in Eastern liturgies and is being studied today thanks to the contributions of several Byzantine scholars of the Pontifical Oriental Institute in Rome. This practice was unknown to the Roman Church. It was unique to the Templars, who seem to have borrowed it from certain ancient popular religious traditions practiced in the city of Jerusalem, perhaps as far back as the early Christian era.

The ritual seems to be connected to the legend of the Holy Grail, the miraculous chalice used by Jesus at the Last Supper to institute the sacrament of the Eucharist, or alternatively, the cup in which Joseph of Arimathea gathered the blood and water that flowed from Christ's pierced side at the crucifixion. This is certainly legitimate speculation, but in the absence of reliable proof a historian must go no further than the simple presentation of the facts. The same consideration applies to the conjecture that the Templars were the custodians of the Shroud of Turin, which was believed to be Jesus' burial shroud. Although there is some evidence to support the theory, proposed some thirty years ago, it isn't conclusive. We know that contemporaries of the Templars considered them the custodians of the most sacred relics of the Passion of Christ, and that in his version of *Parsifal,* the German poet Wolfram von Eschenbach attributed to them the custody of the Grail. New research confirms that this belief may have some basis in truth. Nevertheless, the path to knowledge on this question is still quite long and will lead us to credible results — but only if the search remains distinct from all of the fiction born of utter fantasy that, especially in recent decades, has given the Order of the Knights Templar an exaggeratedly esoteric image. Peter Partner's wonderful book *The Knights Templar and Their Myth* has unmasked similar counterfeits by reconstructing their origins and revealing the economic interests they sometimes conceal.

Another frequently discussed question in the history of the Templars concerns the demise of the order. Clement V's papal bull *Vox in excelso* officially dissolved the order in 1312. This subject is still important today. While there are a number of nonprofit organizations, inspired by the values of the

Templars, that promote laudable cultural and folkloristic initiatives for the public, other groups actually claim to be the heirs of the order, as though it had never been extinguished and survives to this day — despite the last grand master's trial and execution.

The Temple was a religious and military order. Its members were soldiers enlisted in a standing army, bachelors and widowers who took vows of celibacy, obedience, and poverty. How many of today's groups share these fundamental characteristics? Furthermore, there is the insurmountable obstacle of canon law imposed by Clement V, who at the moment he disbanded the order outlawed any attempt whatsoever to resuscitate it without papal consent, going so far as to excommunicate anyone who dared use the name and the symbols of the Temple. It is true that Clement V refused to condemn the order and that his decree dissolving it may be revoked by another pope — yet *Vox in excelso* still stands some seven hundred years later.

Considering the enthusiasm that the subject now enjoys among scholars, readers with a passion for the Templars have much to hope for from future research. Perhaps the proliferation of commercial books about the Templars has actually done the historical profession a great service by piquing popular interest and fueling the demand for further study. If so, then here's to more novels about the Templars and the Holy Grail, especially since there are a good number of young researchers already at work on many still unknown aspects of the order's brief but intense history.

Bibliographic Note

The Templars have been such a popular subject for historians and historical novelists, partly and ironically due to the order's sudden and tragic end, that it is almost impossible to provide an exhaustive bibliography. I have decided, therefore, to cite only publications of unquestionable historical credibility. A similar problem exists for other subjects, such as the rise of medieval knighthood, the crusades, and the history of the papacy from the eleventh to fourteenth century, which are closely related to the history of the Templars. In these cases, I have opted to present a selected bibliographical panorama, giving special attention to the best known and still current works along with the most recent titles.

Any general study of the Templar order must start with the following works: A. Demurger, *Vie et mort de l'ordre du Temple* (Paris, 1985); and M. Barber, *The New Knighthood: A History of the Order of the Temple* (Cambridge, 1994), which cover the entire lifespan of the order. The most useful work on the presumed esoteric offspring of the Temple is P. Partner, *The Murdered Magicians: The*

Templars and Their Myth (Oxford, 1987). Other useful readings include: G. Bordonove, *La vie quotidienne des Templiers au XIIIe siècle* (Paris, 1975); P. Dupuy, *Histoire de l'Ordre Militaire des Templiers* (Brussels, 1751); J. Gmelin, *Schuld und Unschuld des Templerordens* (Stuttgart, 1893); and M. Melville, *La vie des Templiers* (Paris, 1951).

Primary Sources

The main primary sources on the history of the order are the manuscript codices containing the rule and successive constitutions (*rétrais*), the documents contained in the accounts registers of the various Templar houses, and the depositions given by Templar defendants during the trial, which are reported in the records of the inquests that have come down to us.

The most up-to-date critical edition of the Latin and French versions of the rule approved by the Council of Troyes is S. Cerrini, *Une expérience neuve au sein de la spiritualité médiévale: L'Ordre du Temple, 1120–1314. Etude et édition des règles latine et française* is a doctoral dissertation presented in 1998 at the Université Paris IV, Sorbonne. For an overview of the entire body of Templar statutes and regulations reference must be made to the by now outdated edition of H. de Curzon, *La Règle du Temple*, Société de l'Histoire de France (Paris, 1886), as supplemented by the contents of a manuscript published by J. Delaville

Le Roulx, "Un nouveau manuscrit de la Règle du Temple," in *Annuaire-Bulletin de la Société de l'Histoire de France* 26, no. 2 (1889): 185–214. The documents and other information surviving in the Templar house accounts registers are in G. D'Albon, *Cartulaire général de l'Ordre du Temple*, 2 vols. (Paris, 1913–22), which contains a wide repertory of other publications and should be supplemented by G. Léonard, *Introduction au cartulaire manuscrit du Temple, 1150–1317* (Paris, 1930), and the more recent B. A. Lees, *Records of the Templars in England in the Twelfth Century: The Inquest of 1185 with Illustrative Charts and Documents* (Oxford, 1935); and F. Bramato, "L'ordine dei Templari in Italia," in *Nicolaus* 12 (1985). The papal documents related to the early years of the order are in R. Hiestand, *Papsturkunden für Templer und Johanniter*, 3 vols. (Göttingen, 1972–83). The entire corpus of the depositions given by the Templars during the trial has been collected and catalogued in a digital archive as an appendix to B. Frale, *Guardiani del Santuario. Le radici orientali del processo contro l'ordine del Tempio (1129–1314)*, a doctoral dissertation in European social history completed at the History Department of the Ca' Foscari University of Venice, under the supervision of S. Gasparri and G. Ortalli, XI cycle, 2 vols. (Venice, 1996–2000), while the individual primary sources are listed in an appendix to B. Frale, *L'ultima battaglia dei Templari. Dal "codice ombra" d'obbedienza militare alla costruzione del processo per eresia* (Rome, 2001). F. Tommasi, *Interrogatorio di Templari a Cesena, 1310* is an introduction to the published version of the text, in *Acri 1291* (cited below, among the miscellaneous works), pp. 265–300, and the recently discovered record of the Chinon inquest, in B. Frale, *Il Papato e il processo ai Templari: L'inedita assoluzione di Chinon alla luce della diplomatica pontificia* (Rome, 2003), 198–215.

Other important primary sources on the history of the order, although influenced by the particular points of view of their authors, are: the chronicle of William, archbishop of Tyre, Willermi Tyrensis, "Historia rerum in partibus transmarinis gestarum a tempore successorum Mahumet usque ad annum MCLXXXIV," in *Recueil des Historiens des Crusades: Historiens Occidentaux*, 5 vols. (Paris, 1872–95), and the work known as the "Chronicle of the Templar of Tyre," *Chronique du Templier de Tyr*, in *Les Gestes des Chiprois*, ed. Ch. Raynaud, Société de l'Orient Latin Série Historique 5 (Geneva, 1877), 139–334. Most of the pontifical documents dedicated to the Templars have been published in G. Lamattina, *Regesta Pontificum Romanorum erga Templarios, 1139–1313* (Rome, 1984).

Secondary Sources

Miscellaneous works, collections of articles, and conference papers of special interest for the history of the order: *Acri 1291: La fine della presenza degli ordini militari in Terra Santa e i nuovi orientamenti nel XIV secolo*, Biblioteca di

"Militia Sacra" 1, ed. F. Tommasi (Perugia, 1996); *Autour de la prèmiere croisade*, papers from the Conference of the Society for the Study of the Crusades and the Latin East, Clérmont-Ferrand, June 22–25, 1995, ed. M. Malard (Paris, 1996); *Bernardo Cisterciense*, papers from the Twenty-Fifth International History Conference of the Accademia Tudertina Center for the Study of Medieval Spirituality, Todi, October 8–11, 1989 (Perugia, 1990); *De recuperatione Terre Sancte: Dalla "Respublica Christiana" ai primi nazionalismi e alla politica antimediterranea*, ed. A. Diotti (Florence, 1977); *Dei gesta per Francos: Etudes sur les croisades dediées à Jean Richard*, ed. M. Balard, B. Z. Kedar and J. Riley-Smith (Aldershot, 2001); *Die geistlichen Ritterorden Europas*, ed. J. Fleckenstein and M. Hellmann (Sigmaringen, 1980); *Dizionario degli istituti di perfezione*, vol. 1 (Rome, 1974); *Dizionario storico del Papato*, ed. Ph. Levillain, Italian trans. F. Saba Sardi, 2 vols. (Milan, 1996); *Enciclopedia cattolica*, 12 vols. (Rome, 1948–54); *Enciclopedia dei papi*, ed. l'Istituto dell'Enciclopedia Italiana, 3 vols. (Rome, 2000); *Le crociate: L'Oriente e l'Occidente da Urbano II a san Luigi, 1096–1270*, a catalogue of the exhibition held in Rome, Palazzo Venezia, ed. M. Rey-Delqué (Rome, 1997); *Les Croisades*, ed. R. Delort (Paris, 1988); *Les Inquisiteurs: Portraits de défenseur de la foi en Languedoc, XIIIe–XIVe siècles*, ed L. Albaret (Toulouse, 2001); *I laici nella "societas christiana" dei secoli XI e XII*, papers from the Third International Study Week, Mendola, August 21–27, 1965 (Milan, 1968); *I Templari in Piemonte dalla storia al mito*, ed. R. Bordone (Turin, 1995); *I Templari, la guerra e la santità*, ed. S. Cerrini (Rimini, 2000); *I Templari: Mito e storia*, papers delivered at the International Conference at the Templar House in Poggibonsi-Siena, May 29–31, 1987, ed. G. Minnucci and F. Sardi (Sinalunga, 1989); *La Commanderie: Institution des ordres militaires dans l'Occident médiéval*, Premier Colloque International du Conservatoire Larzac Templier et Hospitalier, October 2000 (Paris, 2002); "Lettres des premiers chartreux," *Sources chrétiennes* 88 (Paris, 1962); *Materiali inediti per una storia dei Templari nel Regno di Sicilia*, papers from the Third National "Pavalon" Conference: Workshop of Templar Studies in the Southern Provinces, ed. G. Giordano and C. Guzzo (Manduria, 2002); *La Méditerranée au temps de Saint Louis*, Actes du Colloque d'Aigues-Mortes, April 1997, ed. G. Dédéyan and J. Le Goff (Aigues-Mortes, 1998); *"Militia Christi" e crociata nei secoli XI–XIII*, papers from the Eleventh International Study Week at the Center for Medieval Studies, Mendola, August 28–September 1, 1989 (Milan, 1992); *The Horns of Hattin*, ed. B. Z. Kedar (Jerusalem, 1988); *The Military Orders*, vol. 1, *Fighting for the Faith and Caring for the Sick*, ed. M. Barber (Ashgate, 1994); vol. 2, *Welfare and Warfare*, ed. H. Nicholson (Ashgate, 1998); *Militia sacra. Gli ordini militari tra Europa e Terrasanta*, ed. E. Coli, M. de Marco, and F. Tommasi (Perugia, 1994); *Storici arabi delle crociate*, ed. F. Gabrieli (Turin, 1973); and *Storia della Chiesa*, ed. D. Quaglioni, vol. II, *La crisi del Trecento e il Papato avignonese, 1274–1378* (Turin, 1994).

On the crusades, medieval knighthood, the West's fascination with Eastern civilization, and other subjects connected with the origins of the Temple, a useful overview of the historical literature is provided by P. Alphandéry and A. Dupront, *La Chrétienté et l'Idée de Croisade*, 2 vols. (Paris, 1954); G. Althoff, "Nunc fiant Christi milites, qui dudum extiterunt raptores: Zur Entstehung von Rittertum und Ritterethos," in *Saeculum* 32 (1981): 317–33; A. Barbero, *L'aristocrazia nella società francese del medioevo: Analisi delle fonti letterarie, secoli XI–XIII* (Bologna, 1987); U. R. Blumenthal, "Papal and Local Councils: The Evidence of the 'Pax' and 'Tregua Dei,'" in *La Riforma gregoriana e l'Europa*, in *Studi Gregoriani* 14 (1991): 137–44; M. Bull, *Knightly Piety and the Lay Response to the First Crusade: The Limousin and Gascony, c. 970–c. 1130* (Oxford, 1993); O. Capitani, "Sondaggio sulla terminologia militare in Urbano II," in *"Militia Christi" e Crociata nei secoli XI–XIII*, op. cit., 167–92; F. Cardini, *Alle radici della cavalleria medievale* (Florence, 1981); F. Cardini, "Bernardo e le Crociate," in *Bernardo Cisterciense*, op. cit. 187–97; F. Cardini, *Le crociate tra il mito e la storia* (Rome, 1986); F. Cardini, "La guerra santa nella cristianità," in *"Militia Christi" e Crociata nei secoli XIXIII*, op. cit., 387–99; F. Cardini, *Gerusalemme d'oro, di rame, di luce: pellegrini, crociati, sognatori d'Oriente fra XI e XV secolo* (Milan, 1991); F. Cardini,

"I Cristiani, la guerra e la santità," in *I Templari, la guerra e la santità*, op. cit., 9–17; H. E. J. Cowdrey, "The Peace and the Truce of God in the Eleventh Century," in *Past and Present* 46–49, (1970): 42–67; Cowdrey, *Pope Gregorius VII, 1073–1085* (Oxford, 1998); G. Duby, "Les Origines de la Chevalerie," in *Ordinamenti militari in Occidente nell'alto medioevo*, Fifteenth International Study Week at the Spoleto High Middle Ages Study Center (Spoleto, 1968), 739–61; L. Dupont-Lachenal, "Canonici regolari di S. Agostino," in *Enciclopedia cattolica*, coll. 553–65; J. Flori, *L'Idéologie du glaive: Préhistoire de la chevalerie* (Geneva, 1983); J. Flori, *La première croisade: L'Occident chrétien contre l'Islam (aux origines des ideologies occidentales)* (Brussels, 1992); K. M. Setton, *A History of the Crusades: The First Hundred Years*, vol. 1, ed. M. W. Baldwin (Madison, 1969); and *The Later Crusades (1189–1311)*, vol. 2, ed. R. Lee Wolff and H. W. Hazard (Madison, 1969).

On the main questions of archaeology in the Old and New Testaments: K. M. Kenyon, *Jerusalem: Excavating 3000 Years of History* (London, 1967); F. Cardini, *Il pellegrinaggio: Una dimensione della vita medievale* (Manziana, 1996); A. Frolow, *La relique de la vrai Croix: Recherches sur le développement d'un culte* (Paris, 1961); J. B. Segal, *Edessa the Blessed City* (Oxford, 1970); and E. Wilson, *The Scrolls of the Dead Sea* (London, 1955).

On the birth of the Templar order, papal approval of the rule, the role of Bernard of Clairvaux, and questions related to the rule: F. Cardini, *I poveri cavalieri del Cristo.*

Bernardo di Clairvaux e la fondazione dell'ordine templare (Rimini, 1992); T. di Carpegna Falconieri, "Innocenzo II," in *Enciclopedia dei Papi*, op. cit., 261–68; S. Cerrini, "Onorio II," in *Enciclopedia dei Papi*, op. cit., 255–58; S. Cerrini, "Celestino II," in *Enciclopedia dei Papi*, op. cit., 259–61; S. Cerrini, "I Templari: Una vita da fratres, ma una regola anti-ascetica; una vita da cavalieri, ma una regola anti-eroica," in *I Templari, la guerra e la santità*, op. cit., 19–48; S. Cerrini, "A New Edition of the Latin and French Rule of the Temple," in *The Military Orders: Welfare and Warfare*, op. cit., 207–15; S. Cerrini, "L'ordine del Tempio: Aggiornamento bibliografico," in *I Templari, la guerra e la santità*, op. cit., 153–63; S. Cerrini, "Le Fondateur de l'ordre du Temple à ses frères: Hugues de Payns et le 'Sermo Christi militibus,'" in *Dei gesta per Francos: Etudes sur les croisades dediées à Jean Richard*, op. cit., 99–110; R. Hiestand, "Kardinalbischof Matthäus von Albano, das Konzil von Troyes und die Entstehung des Templerordens," in *Zeitschrift für Kirchengeschichte* 99 (1980): 17–37; K. Körner, *Die Tempelregel. Aus dem Altfranzösischen übersetzt und mit erläuternden Anmerkungen versehen* (Jena, 1904); F. Tommasi, "'Pauperes commilitones Christi': Aspetti e problemi delle origini gerosolimitane," in *"Militia Cristi" e Crociata nei secoli XI–XIII*, op. cit., 443–75; F. Tommasi, "Per i rapporti tra Templari e Cisterciensi: Orientamenti e indirizzi di ricerca," in *I Templari: Una vita tra riti cavallereschi e fedeltà alla Chiesa*, papers from the First Conference "I Templari e san Bernardo di Chiaravalle," Certosa di

Firenze, October 23–24, 1992, 227–74; K. Elm, "Kanoniker und Ritter vom Heiligen Grab: Ein Beitrag zur Entstehung und Frügeschichte der palästinischen Ritterorden," in *Die geistlichen Ritterorden Europas*, op. cit., 141–69; K. Elm, "Canonici del Tempio," in *Dizionario degli Istituti di Perfezione*, coll. 884–86; J. Leclerq, "Un document sur les débuts des Templiers," in *Revue d'histoire ecclésiastique* 52 (1957): 81–91; G. Ligato, "Fra Ordini Cavallereschi e crociata: 'Milites ad Terminum' e 'confraternitates' armate," in *"Militia Christi" e Crociata nei secoli XI–XIII*, op. cit., 645–53; D. Selwood, "'Quidam autem dubitaverunt': The Saint, the Sinner, the Temple, and a Possible Chronology," in *Autour de la première croisade*, op. cit., 221–30; F. Tommasi, "I Templari e il culto delle reliquie," in *I Templari: mito e storia*, op. cit., 191–210; and J. M. Upton-Ward, "The Rule of the Templars," in *Studies in the History of Medieval Religion* 4 (1997).

Some interesting new findings have been proposed in the recent study by L. Pavanello, *Da "fraternitas" a "ordo": ragioni per la fondazione di una "militia," i "Pauperes commilitones Christi,"* a thesis presented to the History Department of the Ca' Foscari University of Venice, 2004, and in a recent study of the Templars in Sicily by C. Guzzo, *Templari in Sicilia: La storia e le sue fonti tra Federico II e Roberto d'Angiò* (Genoa, 2003).

On the individual grand masters of the order see: M. Barber, "James de Molay: The Last Grand Master of the Temple," in *Studia Monastica* 14 (1972): 91–124; M. L.

Bulst-Thiele, *Sacrae Domus Militiae Templi Hyerosolimitani Magistri: Untersuchungen zur Geschichte des Templerordens, 1118/19–1314* (Göttingen, 1974); A. Demurger, *Jacques de Molay: Le crépuscule des templiers* (Paris, 2002); P. Duguyet, *Essai sur Jacques de Molay* (Paris, 1906); A. Forey, "Letters of the Two Last Templar Masters," in *Nottingham Medieval Studies* 45 (2001): 145–71; T. Leroy, *Hugues de Payns, chevalier champenois, fondateur de l'Ordre des Templiers* (Troyes, 2001); G. Lizérand, "Les Dépositions du grand maître Jacques de Molay au procès des templiers, 1307–1314," in *Le Moyen âge* 26 (1913): 81–106; J. Philips, "Hugues of Payens and the 1129 Damascus Crusade," in *The Military Orders*, vol. 1, op. cit., 141–47; W. Schwarz, "Die Schuld des Jakob von Molay, des letzten Grossmeister des Templer," in *Welt als Geschichte* 17 (1957): 259–79; V. Thomassin, *Figures comtoises: Jacques de Molay* (Paris, 1912); and A. Trunz, *Zur Geschichte des letzten Templermeister* (Freiburg, 1919).

On the Temple's military role and the problems involved in defending the Holy Land: M. Barber, "Supplying the Crusaders States: The Role of the Templars," in *The Horns of Hattin*, op. cit.; A. Demurger, "Templiers et hospitaliers dans le combat de Terre sainte," in *Le Combattant au Moyen Âge*, ed. M. Balard (Paris, 1995): 77–96; A. Demurger, *Chevaliers du Christ: Les ordres religieux-militaires au Moyen Âge, XIe–XVIe siècle* (Paris, 2002); C. Gaier, "Armes et combats dans l'universe médiéval," in *Bibliothèque du Moyen âge* 5 (1995); A. Forey, "Novitiate and Instruction in the Military Orders during the Twelfth and

Thirteenth Centuries," in *Speculum* 61 (1986); A. Forey, *The Military Orders: From the Twelfth to the Early Fourteenth Centuries* (London, 1992); A. Forey, "Gli ordini militari e la difesa degli stati crociati," in *Le Crociate: L'Oriente e l'Occidente*, op. cit., 253–58; A. Luttrell, "Templari e Ospitalieri: alcuni confronti," in *I Templari, la guerra e la santità*, op. cit., 133–52; C. Marshall, *Warfare in the Latin East, 1192–1291* (Cambridge, 1992); H. Nicholson, *Templars, Hospitallers, and Teutonic Knights: Images of the Military Orders, 1128–1291* (London, 1995); C. Prawer, *Histoire du royaume latin de Jérusalem*, 2 vols. (Paris, 1969–70); D. Pringle, "Templar Castles between Jaffa and Jerusalem," in *The Military Orders*, op. cit., 2: 89–109; D. Pringle, "Templar Castles on the Road of the Jordan," in ibid., 1: 148–66; J. Riley-Smith, "The Templars and Teutonic Knights in Cilician Armenia," in *The Cilician Kingdom of Armenia*, ed. T. S. R. Boase (Edinburgh, 1978): 92–117; and S. Runciman, *A History of the Crusades*, 3 vols. (Cambridge, 1951, 1952, 1954).

On the order's financial activities: L. Delisle, "Mémoires sur les opérations financières des Templiers," in *Mémoires de l'Institut National de France, Académie des Inscription et Belles-Lettres* 33 (Paris, 1889); A. Demurger, "Trésor des templiers, trésor du roi: Mise au point sur les opérations financiers des templiers," in *Pouvoir et Gestion* 5 (1997): 73–85; L. Di Fazio, *Lombardi e Templari nella realtà socio-economica durante il regno di Filippo il Bello, 1285–1314* (Milan, 1986); D. M. Metcalf, "The Templars as Bankers and Monetary Transfers between West and East in the Twelfth Century," in *Coinage in the Latin East: The Fourth Oxford Symposium on Coinage and Monetary History*, ed. P. W. Edbury and D. M. Metcalf (Oxford, 1980); and J. Piquet, *Des Banquiers au moyen âge: Les Templiers* (Paris, 1939).

On the opposition to the military orders in the second half of the thirteenth century, proposals to merge the orders, and the end of the Christian states in the Holy Land: P. Amargier, "La défense du Temple devant le concile de Lyon en 1274," in *1274, année charnière: Mutations et continuité*, Colloque international du Cnrs, Lyon-Paris 1974 (Paris, 1977): 495–501; F. Cardini, "Il ruolo degli ordini militari nel progetto di 'recuperatio' della Terrasanta secondo la trattatistica dalla fine del XIII al XIV secolo," in *Acri 1291*, op. cit., 137–42; A. Demurger, "Les Templiers, Matthieu Paris et les sept péchés capitaux," in *I Templari: Mito e storia*, op. cit., 153–69; Demurger, "Les Ordres militaires et la croisade au début du XIVe siècle: Quelques remarques sur les traités de croisade de Jacques de Molay et Foulques de Villaret," in *Dei gesta per Francos: Etudes sur les croisades dediées à Jean Richard*, op. cit.; M. L. Favreau-Lilie, "The Military Orders and the Escape of the Christian Population from the Holy Land in 1291," in *Journal of Medieval History* 19, no. 3 (1993): 201–27; P. Edbury, "The Templars in Cyprus," in *The Military Orders*, op. cit., 1: 189–95; P. Riant, "Etudes sur les derniers temps du royaume de Jérusalem," in *Archives de l'Orient Latin* 14 (1878);

and B. Z. Kedar and S. Schein, "Un projet de passage particulier proposé par l'Ordre de l'Hôpital, 1306–1307," in *Bibliothèque de l'École des Chartes* 137 (1979): 212–26. On the Templars' spirituality and their special liturgies: M. L. Bulst, "Noch einmal das Itinerarium peregrinorum," in *Deutsches Archiv für Erforschung des Mittelalters* 20 (1964): 210–21; C. Dondi, "Manoscritti liturgici dei Templari e degli Ospitalieri: Le nuove prospettive aperte dal sacramentario templare di Modena (Biblioteca capitolare O. II. 13)," in *I Templari, la guerra e la santità*, op. cit., 85–131; K. Elm, "Die Spiritualität der geistlichen Ritterdorden des Mittelalters: Forschungsstand und Forschungsprobleme," in *"Militia Christi" e Crociata*, op. cit., 477–518; B. Frale, "Chevaliers d'Outremer: Note di ricerca sugli esordi dell'ordine templare fra Occidente e Terrasanta," in *EVKOSMIA: Studi miscellanei per il 75° di Vincenzo Poggi S.I.*, ed. V. Ruggieri and L. Pieralli (Catanzaro, 2003): 257–74; J. Leclerq, "Un document sur les débuts des Templiers," in *Revue d'histoire ecclésiastique* 52 (1957); A.-M. Legras and J.-L. Lemaître, "La pratique liturgique des Templiers et des Hospitaliers de Saint-Jean de Jerusalem," in *L'écrit dans la société medievale*, essays in honor of Lucie Fossier (Paris, 1991): 77–137; H. E. Mayer, "Zum Itinerarium peregrinorum: Eine Erwiderung," in *Deutsches Archiv für Erforschung des Mittelalters* 21 (1965): 593–606; H. E. Mayer, "Zur Verfasserfrage des Itinerarium peregrinorum," in *Classica et medievalia* 26 (1965): 279–92; F. Tommasi, "I

Templari e il culto delle reliquie," in *I Templari: mito e storia*, op. cit., 191–210. On the conflict between the papacy and the French crown surrounding the question of the Templars: R. H. Bautier, "Diplomatique et histoire politique: Ce que la critique diplomatique nous apprend sur la personnalité de Philippe le Bel," in *Revue historique* 259 (1978); M. Boutaric, "Clement V, Philippe le Bel et les Templiers, I^e partie," in *Revue des questions historiques* 10 (1871); J. Bernard, "Le népotisme de Clément V et ses complaisances pour la Gascogne," in *Annales du Midi* 61 (1949): 369–412; M.-D. Chenu, "Dogme et théologie dans la bulle 'Unam sanctam,'" in *Recherches de science religieuse* 40 (1952): 307–16; J. Coste, *Boniface VIII en process: Articles d'accusation et dépositions des témoins, 1303–1311* (Rome, 1995); M. Delle Piane, "La disputa tra Filippo il Bello e Bonifacio VIII," in *Storia delle idee politiche, economiche e sociali*, ed. L. Firpo, 2 vols. (Turin, 1983): 497–541; M. C. De Matteis, "La Chiesa verso un modello teocratico: da Gregorio VII a Bonifacio VIII," in *La Storia: I grandi problemi dal Medioevo all'Età contemporanea*, ed. N. Tranfaglia and M. Firpo, vol. 1, *Il Medioevo: I quadri generali* (Turin, 1988): 425–52; A. Demurger, "Benedetto XI," in *Dizionario storico del Papato*, op. cit., 161–62; Demurger, "Clemente V," in ibid., 325–27; J. H. Denton, "Pope Clement V's Early Career as a Royal Clerk," in *The English Historical Review* 83 (1968): 303–14; Y. Dossat, "Guillaume de Nogaret, petit-fils d'hérétique," in *Annales du Midi* 53 (1941): 391–402; E. Dupré Theseider, "Bonifacio VIII," in *Enciclopedia dei papi*, op. cit., 472–93; J. Favier, *Philippe le Bel* (Paris, 1978); R. Fawtier, "L'attentat d'Anagni," in *Mélanges d'archeologie et d'histoire* 60 (1948): 153–79; H. Finke, *Acta Aragonensia: Quellen zur deutschen, italienischen, französischen, spanischen, zur Kirchen und Kulturgeschichte aus der diplomatischen Korrespondenz Jayme II, 1291–1327*, 3 vols. (Berlin-Leipzig, 1908–22); B. Guillemain, *La cour pontificale d'Avignon (1309–1376): Etude d'une société* (Paris, 1962); Guillemain, "Bonifacio VIII e la teocrazia pontificia," in *Storia della Chiesa*, op. cit., 129–74; Guillemain, "Il papato sotto la pressione del re di Francia," in ibid., 177–232; P. Herde, "Celestino V," in ibid., 93–127; Ch.-V. Langlois, "Documents rélatifs à Bertrand de Got (Clément V)," in *Revue historique* 60 (1889): 48–54; G. Lizérand, *Clément V et Philippe le Bel* (Paris, 1910); R. Manselli, "Arnaldo da Villanova e i Papi del suo tempo," in *Studi Romani* 7 (1959): 146–61; M. Melville, "Guillaume de Nogaret et Philip le Bel," in *Revue d'histoire de l'Eglise de France* 36 (1950): 56–66; S. Menache, "Clément V et le royaume de France: Un nouveau régard," in *Revue d'histoire de l'Eglise de France* 74 (1988): 23–38; A. Paravicini Bagliani, "Clemente V," in *Enciclopedia dei papi*, op. cit., 501–12; P. Dubois, *De recuperatione Terrae Sanctae* (Paris, 1891); A. Rigault, "Le procès de Guichard, évêque de Troyes, 1308–1313," in *Mémoires et documents publiés par la Société de l'Ecole des Chartes* 1 (Paris, 1886); T. Schmidt, "Papst Bonifaz VIII und die Idolatrie," in *Quellen und Forschungen aus italiani-*

schen Archiven und Bibliotheken 66 (1986): 75–107; T. Schmidt, *Der Bonifaz-Prozess: Verfahren der Papstanklage in der Zeit Bonifaz VIII und Clemens V* (Cologne, 1989); J. R. Strayer, *The Reign of Philip the Fair* (Princeton, N.J., 1980); L. Thomas, "La vie privée de Guillaume de Nogaret," in *Annales du Midi* 16 (1904): 161–207; L. Viollet, "Berenger Fredol, canoniste," in *Histoire litteraire de la France* 34 (1915): 62–178; J. L. Villanueva, *Viage literario á las Iglesias de España* (Madrid, 1806) 5: 207–21; *Vitae Paparum Avenionensium*, ed. M. Mollat, 4 vols. (Paris, 1914–27); and I. Walter, "Benedetto XI," in *Enciclopedia dei papi*, op. cit., 493–500.

On the events of the trial, the Inquisition, the Council of Vienne, and the burning at the stake of the last grand master: M. C. Barber, *The Trial of the Templars* (Cambridge, 1978); Bernardi Guidonis, *Practica inquisitionis heretice pravitatis*, ed. C. Douais (Paris, 1886); M. L. Bulst-Thiele, "Der Prozess gegen den Templerorden," in *Die geistlichen Ritterorden Europas*, op. cit.; R. Caravita, *Rinaldo da Concorezzo, arcivescovo di Ravenna (1303–1321) al tempo di Dante* (Florence, 1964); C. R. Cheney, "The Downfall of the Templars and a Letter in Their Defence," in *Medieval Miscellany Presented to Eugène Vinaver*, ed. F. Whitehead, A. M. Divernes, and F. E. Sutcliffe (Manchester, 1965): 65–79; "Chronique rimée attribuée à Geoffroy de Paris," in *Revue Historique des Gaules et de la France* 22 (1865): 87–166; K. Elm, "Il processo dei Templari 1307–1312," in *Acri 1291*, op. cit., 213–25; H. Finke, *Papsttum und*

Untergang des Templerordens, 2 vols. (Münster, 1907); *Portraits de défenseur de la foi en Languedoc, XIIIe–XIVe siècle*, ed. L. Albaret (Toulouse, 2001); Ch. Lea, *A History of the Inquisition of the Middle Ages*, 3 vols. (New York, 1888–89); F. Liuzzi, "Apostasia," in *Enciclopedia cattolica*, op. cit., coll. 1674–75; G. Lizérand, *Le Dossier de l'affaire des Templiers* (Paris, 1923; rev. ed. 1964); G. G. Merlo, *Eretici ed eresie medievali* (Bologna, 1989); E. Müller, *Das Konzil von Vienne, 1311–1312: Seine Quelle und seine Geschichte* (Münster, 1934); H. Prutz, *Entwicklung und Untergang des Templerherrenordens* (Berlin, 1888); M. Raynouard, *Monuments historiques relatifs à la condamnation des Chevaliers du Temple* (Paris, 1813); S. Reinach, "La Tête magique des Templiers," in *Revue de l'histoire des religions* 63 (1911): 25–39; J. M. Sansterre, "Formoso," in *Enciclopedia dei papi*, op. cit., 41–47; K. Schottmüller, *Der Untergang des Templerordens*, 2 vols. (Berlin, 1887); A. Sennis, "Giovanni VIII," in *Enciclopedia dei papi*, op. cit., 28–34; R. Sève and A. M. Chagny Sève, *Le procès des Templiers d'Auvergne* (Paris, 1986); H. D. Simonin, "La notion d' 'intentio' dans l'oeuvre de St. Thomas d'Aquin," in *Revue des sciences philosophiques et théologiques* 19 (1930): 455–63; L. Van Leinwen, "L'intention et son object," in *Mélanges philosophiques*, vol. 2 (Amsterdam, 1948): 122–31; I. E. Van Roey, "Disquisitio de axiomate: 'Non sunt facienda mala ut eveniant bona,'" in *La vie diocésaine* 2 (1980): 114–20; and G. Zannoni, "Eresia," in *Enciclopedia cattolica*, op. cit., coll. 487–93.

On the secret induction ceremony: B. Frale, *L'ultima*

battaglia dei Templari: Dal "codice ombra" d'obbedienza militare alla costruzione del processo per eresia, op. cit.

On the papal absolution granted to the leaders of the order: B. Frale, "Un nuovo documento sul processo dei Templari," in *Materiali inediti per una storia dei Templari*, op. cit., 49–58; B. Frale, "The Chinon Charter: Papal Absolution to Last Templar Master Jacques de Molay," in *Journal of Medieval History* 30 (2004): 109–34; and B. Frale, "Il Papato e il processo dei Templari: L'inedita assoluzione di Chinon alla luce della diplomatica pontificia," in *La corte dei papi*, op. cit.

Index